Carousel of Dreams

Larry Leonard Fleischer
and Rita J. Fleischer

Summer 1997

1st printing 2011

2nd printing 2020

Print ISBN 979-8-6472-3079-9

Poems by Larry L Fleischer

Layout, design, photos & Story by Rita J. Fleischer

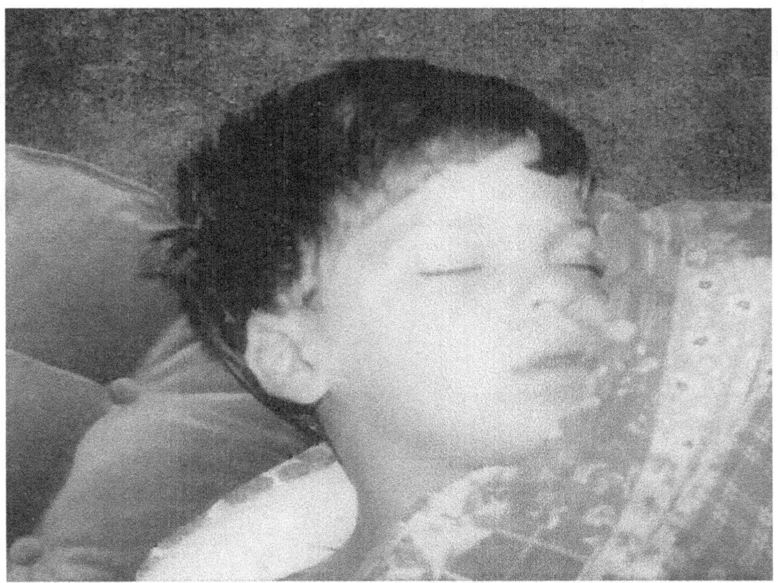

This book is dedicated to our beloved son who was taken from this world to soon

May he rest in piece

A big Thank You to everyone who tried to help me with the word program since I am not very "Teci" as it became quite a project getting this submitted. Also, to my beautiful girls just for being you and being there for me after the loss of your brother and dad. It has been difficult going on without my soul mate. To my terrific son-in-law's for making my girls happy and for being such wonderful family men. You have been so great to have around during the holidays with all your wonderful cooking skills. And to all my wonderful grandchildren who have been an inspiration and have turned out to be such kind and loving human beings. I am so proud of all of you and all that you have accomplished. I love you all so very much. This story is for you.

xoxo Mom/Nana

Table of Contents

Shattered   ~   By Erik Fleischer

**This rendering shows the mental anguish
and turmoil within himself**

On June 28th at twenty-five years old, Erik took his life after seven years of struggling with the mental condition schizophrenia.   And that would forever change the lives of his family. Erik was struck down in the prime of life with an illness incurable and so destructive, one cannot even imagine the incredible mental pain he suffered with every day: unable to be with his friends because of the symptoms and disturbing images, being afraid people could see something was wrong, becoming more and more isolated, robbing him of the joy and happiness we all deserve as human beings, the loneliness becoming unbearable. Out of this devastating event came the inspiring poems written by his father. It has become a source of healing not only for him and his family but an inspiration to others who have endured the great pain of losing a child. He is gone but our family needed a place to tend the great love for him that remains. The poems show that love, as well as the pain, guilt, forgiveness, and the struggle to go on without him.

Love at First Sight

This is not your typical love story where boy meets girl, falls in love and they live happily ever after. This love story is about love and the unbearable loss of a child and the bond to continue without their son as well as the love to continue on together despite that loss.

It was March 1, 1963 when I was dropped off at Art Center in Pasadena for an art class my parents had signed me up for. I was 15 at the time. The classroom was set up with a model dressed up as a clown and a semicircle of chairs around him. As I got seated, I looked around at the other students and I noticed an attractive guy on the other side of the room. At the break, several girls surrounded him to admire his work. When they walked away, I went over to see what the fuss was about. Sure, enough his drawing was remarkable. Much better than mine. He seemed shy and modest about his work. We walked out to the coffee truck to talk.

I was very attracted to him, with his olive complexion, dark wavy hair, and the most beautiful green eyes I had ever seen. After the class ended and we walked out together, I waited for him to ask for my phone number, but he never did so, I asked him for his number, mentioning maybe we could get together sometime. Now, at 15 back in 1963 that was quite a bold move. But I was smitten and was not going to lose out on getting to know this guy.

The Phone Call and The Prom

The next day my little sister and I decided to go roller skating, a great pastime in those days. Upon returning home that day, my mom said, "A Larry called". It was him. I was so Excited. I called him back, stretching the wall phone cord, sitting on the kitchen floor resting against the door. We talked for hours. About what, I do not remember, but we just clicked. Turns out he was a Senior at Culver High and was graduating in June. I was only a Sophomore at South High School in Torrance. Our first date was going miniature golfing. We dated steadily for several months and he asked me to his prom. I was so honored to be his date. I wore a pale green long strapless gown with ruffles from the top to the bottom. It was held at a country club nearby. The music was dreamy as we danced the night away. At the break we walked outside around the grounds and he kissed me under the moonlight. It was so romantic. The connection was clear.

Larry's Prom ~ May 2003

Meeting the Parents

I knew I was in love. We went to the movies and a dance at my school called the Thai Ling. We spent the day at Pacific Ocean Park, taking a photo behind a painted board of a merman and mermaid holding hands.

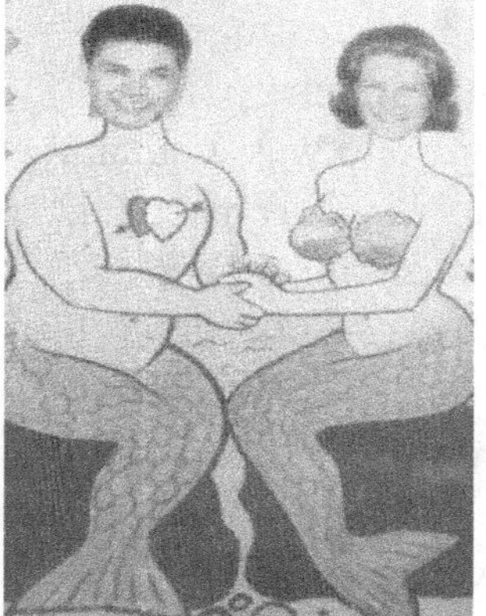

The cutest picture ever. Sadly, the park is no longer there all these years later. These were the days of Peter Paul & Mary, the Beach Party movies with Frankie and Annette, Cleopatra the movie and The Beverly Hillbillies on T.V. A carefree and innocent time of life in America. It was at this time we saw the movie "A Summer Place" with Troy Donahue and Sandra Dee and adopted our song "A Theme from a Summer Place." It was our song forever and whenever we heard it played Larry would take me in his arms and dance with me. It always brought tears to my eyes.

He was always romantic. It was around this time my parents wanted to meet his parents and was invited to stop by one Sunday afternoon.

Larry and I went off talking and I signed his yearbook while the parents visited. My mother was very racially prejudiced and because Larry looked like he could be Mexican, she wanted to see for herself. He is mostly German, Spanish and a small part Mexican. I thought he was so handsome, and I was wildly crazy about him.

Larry Graduates - 1963

But when she met his mom and sister, it was obvious that the Spanish/Mexican nationality was prominent. His biological father was all German. His mother and sister had the exotic look of the Spanish side.

In June we attended his Graduation. He was given a scholarship to the Art Center of Design because of his great artistic talent. I was so proud of him.

The Move

      I had just entered my Jr. year and was set to try out to become a song leader when my parents announced that we were moving from Torrance to Thousand Oaks, quite a bit farther from Larry. I cannot help but feel this was on purpose to break us up. She just could not accept the relationship due to her prejudicial thinking. So off we went to a new school, my having to hustle to make new friends and campaign to become a part of Thousand Oaks High's song leader squad. Larry went on to college studying his art, in hopes to someday work for the Disney Studios. Since he did not have a car and had to borrow his stepdads, he could not come out and see me often. We managed to keep in touch. We even had his family out for Thanksgiving that year. I was asked to be in his sister Joan's wedding in the spring of 1964. After that we saw each other only a few

times and eventually lost touch. I had been nominated to be on the squad, my dream since my freshman year. So, my summer was spent going to cheerleading camp and learning routines. And in the fall were the football and

basketball games that I was a part of. I had so much fun. And Larry was busy with his college and taking part in his activities. We did not see each other anymore. It was my Senior year and I did not date much, to begin with anyway.

Proposal, Graduation & A Wedding

The following events would change the course of my life forever!

My parents had gotten me a horse the year before, which I loved going out and riding. He was stabled at a nearby facility in Thousand Oaks. However, it seemed the guys, including Larry, did not care to ride. Since I was going into my Senior year and would not have a lot of time to ride, I decided to sell him. I rode my horse to the nearest feed store where I was going to post a picture on their bulletin board. When coming out of the store to get on my horse and ride home, this guy pulled up in the parking lot in his little sports car, got out and started walking toward me, proceeding to ask me out. Now I was only 16 at the time, and he looked a lot older. The rules of the house were my parents had to meet anyone I dated first. I told him that and he said ok, giving me his number. He was so good looking and tall. My girlfriend Jackie lived nearby so I rode over to her house before going home to tell her about the meeting. Turns out she knew him and said she grew up with him and that he lived down the street. She gave me a warning saying I should not date him. But I did not listen, and we had him over for dinner, having no idea how old he was. While sitting around the table having dinner, my brother says "Hey, how old are you?" And he responds with "21." Personally, I think that was too old for a sixteen-year old girl, but the go ahead was given to date him. I was flattered he liked me, so we dated and had a good time. I was attracted to him but I am not sure it was really love, because at that age you really do not know what love is about. I would say more like lust at that age and he had been around the block a few times, so they say. I turned 17 in November and one day shortly after, he asked me to marry him. No ring just asked.

That day we came in to tell Mom, dad was on a flight and not home. She was thrilled since she was married by the Justice of the Piece and wanted to plan a nice wedding for me, the oldest. Plus, I think she felt I would be safe in a marriage and not dating. In those days, a career was not talked about. I was to marry and have a family and be a homemaker like she was. She grabbed the calendar to set a date.

She did not feel we should date through the summer and said we should have the wedding the Saturday after graduation. I graduated on a Thursday and was married on that Saturday, two days later.

Oh, and she informed him that he should have a ring by January because she wanted to have an engagement party. My girlfriend Jackie was also engaged so she had the party for both of us. I broke it off a few months later saying I felt I was too young to get married. I would not be 18 until the following November. But somehow Mom got us back together. It seems that most of my girlfriends were getting married, so I went ahead. Dad flew us in his plane to Catalina for our honeymoon, which was nice, but we only had the weekend since my husband had been laid off and needed to look for a new job. So, we lived on the wedding money we received.

Surprise its Twins!

Being the homemaker, I was raised to be, the next step was a baby. I had loved the Shirley Temple movies and especially the one where she played Heidi. I decided that was going to be the name of my first baby if it was a girl. I became pregnant in May, eleven months after getting married. It turned out my girlfriend Jackie, who was in my wedding and I was in hers, gave birth to twins three months before I was due, and she had twin boys. I went over to her house and the babies were both crying and there was the smell of dirty diapers in the air. I said, "Jackie I'd just die if I had twins!" I had made a pretty bassinet with a pink ruffled skirt around it in hopes we would have a girl. I wanted one so bad. I was due in January but on December 21st while visiting a neighbor, I stood up and my water broke all over their floor. The women knew what was happening and told me to call the doctor, of which he said to get into his office right away and he would check me out. I met my husband there and after the doctor examined me, he said there were two! I could not believe it! He was a country doctor and did not hear two heart beats through his stethoscope. He said he would have to have listened through my back to hear both heartbeats. Meanwhile I am cramping bad, so we were sent to the hospital right away.

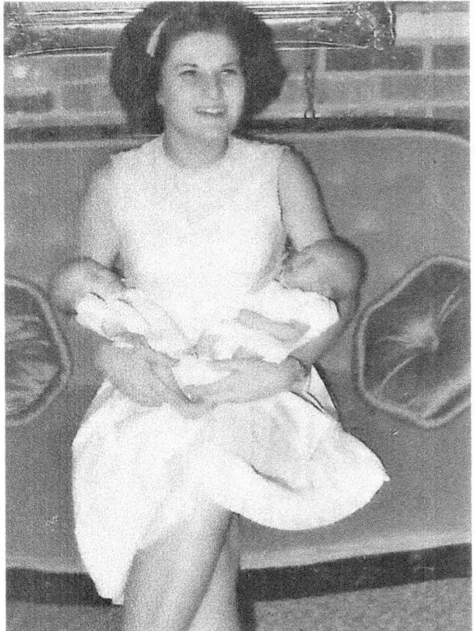

It was 3pm when we arrived and at 9:00 and 9:01 we had two beautiful little girls. Baby #1 was of course Heidi and the 2nd became Holli for the Christmas Season plus it matched. I came home Christmas Eve but since they were under 5lbs they had to stay a few days in the hospital. What a Christmas present! I was thrilled. That is what I get for wishing so hard for a girl, I got two! Being only 19 at the time, it was quite a responsibility.

Moving Home

Due to many unhappy events in the marriage after three years, I decided to file for divorce, asking my mom if I could move back home. Her remark was "I expected this, just not this soon." (Then why did you push me into this marriage, I thought). So, at 21 I was a single mother and was expected to find another husband, not go to school or work at a job, just find another husband! I dated a few people and my sister babysat, bless her heart, but there was no one I saw even remotely that I wanted. Poor dad, he was on a flight when my brother helped me move home, filling the garage with my things. When he arrived home and opened the garage, he saw it was full of my furniture and knew what had happened. But he never said anything. What a guy! This was 1968 and for 10 months I dated with no luck of making any connection with anyone I liked. At least, well enough to marry. Some were crazy about me and were willing to take on two toddlers, but I had to be the one who felt something with them and just had not met anyone I felt "crazy" about.

Love at First Sight....Again!

It's now spring of 1969 and my parents had gone to a party when I put the girls to bed and I sat down to look through my souvenirs from high school, when I came across the wedding invitation of Larry's sister, the wedding I was in back in 1964, so long ago. On that invitation was his Stepfather's last name. I knew what Larry's last name was but did not remember his Stepfather's. I grabbed the phone book to look the name up and sure enough it was the only one listed. I did not hesitate to dial the number. Recognizing Larry's moms voice, I told her who I was. Really surprised, she said "Larry's here, do you want to talk to him?" Did I ever! It was like no time had passed at all. We picked up where we left off, except now I was a blond and had two-year old twins. Last he saw me I had dark auburn hair and was 16. Turns out he graduates from college in June. He said when the Viet Nam war came along, he had to change from Art to Business since Art did not qualify for a deferment and he did not believe in the war and did not want to go. So sad since he would have made a wonderful artist. I had butterflies in my stomach just talking to him. I asked if he wanted to come over and he said he would love to see me again after all these years, six to be exact. At this point my parents had moved back to the area, except to Play Del Rey in a home overlooking the ocean. The front doors of this house were two large tall double doors. As you entered there was the master bedroom to the left and the formal dining room and kitchen ahead and to the right was the living room with floor to ceiling windows overlooking the ocean. I had put the girls to bed in the downstairs bedroom. There was a knock at the door, I was so nervous wondering how he looked after all this time. Opening the door, I was not disappointed. He looked better than ever. He was awfully thin at 17 and now he had filled out and looked more mature. I could tell the attraction was still there. He was fascinated with my blond hair and said he really liked it. About this time after talking a bit, up came the girls to investigate (Drat, they were supposed to stay in bed!) He summoned them over and talked to them.

He seemed to like them. (phew!) It was getting late, after putting the girls down again, I walked him out to the car. It was cool out, but I was so nervous I was shivering, because of that rather than the cold. I said, "I'd better go in" and turned to walk away when he stopped me with his arm and drew me in for a kiss! I swear I heard fireworks go off. We were like two magnets. The same feelings, only stronger.

The Proposal

We dated through the summer after I attended his Graduation from College, having been there for his High School Graduation, like no time had passed. We were crazy about each other. Then one day when we were kidding around, I made a statement to him "I thought you were going to ask me to marry you" and he said, "you would?" Kind of sneaky turning the tables on him that way, I guess. Sometimes, guys need a little help in that department, I think. I was sure he felt the same way and knew it was good. I said, yes, yes, yes! We could not imagine our lives without each other. And he was so good with the girls. A natural father, I felt. He was so kind and loving to all of us. I could see a bright future with him in it. His only question to me was would I be willing to have more children? There was no doubt that I wanted to have a baby with this man. His gorgeous dark wavy hair and green eyes, that were sure to turn out beautiful children. To my mother's relief, even though six years earlier she did not want me to marry him, he has come along to marry me now and wanted to be a father to my two little girls. All was good with the world!

Larry Graduates College - 1969

The Wedding and Honeymoon

After graduation, Larry got a job with an Insurance Company and we could start to plan our wedding. It was set for February 7, 1970. We had 100 guests in the Star of Creation Chapel in Los Angeles. The ceiling was sections of blue glass causing the sky to shine through as we said our vows promising to love each other forever. I made my gown from a pale pink material with a lace overlay on top and lace sleeves down to the wrist with small satin buttons. The vail was of the same lace. Larry never did forgive me for not wearing white since this was his first marriage, but back then in the 70's when you had children and were remarrying, it just wasn't done. We had the reception at my parent's home overlooking the ocean. It really was lovely. Larry's father came as well as his mother and stepfather. Joan, his sister, was one of my bridesmaids and I made her dress and my sisters with a red velvet top and the same pale pink material on the skirt portion. My girlfriend, Fran, was my maid of honor and wore a solid red velvet dress, which she made. Since Larry was new at his job, he could not take time off, so we decided to drive to Palm Springs for a one-night Honeymoon. The mistake we made was not making reservations. The Bob Hope Classic was going on and there was not a room in sight. By this time, it was quite late and driving back to an outlying town, it was very dark in the desert. Suddenly we found ourselves skidding in the gravel in the center divider area. The car stalled and would not start. The car we had was a little blue VW and rocks had flown up in-to the engine. We did not know what we were going to do. It was around 11:00 at night and very dark out. Fortunately, a police car came along a few minutes later and he gave us a ride to the nearest open establishment. From there we called a cab to take us to a hotel in Redlands with our luggage and two bottles of champagne. What a night! We had a wonderful romantic evening. How did I get so lucky? The next day we had the car towed and repaired, taking most of the money we had brought with us. But we wanted to drive back into Palm Springs and have a nice lunch at least. Suddenly while there we realized we had left my dress and his suit at the hotel in Redlands. What else could go wrong? We called ahead and stopped by to pick up our clothes and headed home to pick up the girls and go to our new apartment in Alhambra, ready to start life as Mr. and Mrs.

now for the honeymoon

Setting Up Housekeeping

We had furnished our new place with a lot of hand me downs from family as most young couples do. We were given a big brown couch from his family, a gold leafed oval coffee table from mine, maple end tables and lamps and a kitchenette with turquoise chairs. The first night when Larry came home from work, I had the table set with candles and flowers and dinner ready. The girls were dressed and looked adorable and of course I was wearing a dress with an apron on like you would see in the 50's. He was so pleased when we all came up to greet him with kisses and hugs. Life was complete at last.

My First Job

Six months later, Larry was laid off and I needed to find a job. I had never worked before, so this was going to be a new experience for me. I decided to sign up with a temporary help service to begin with. They sent me out on various jobs such as carrying a tray around of perfumes offering customers a sample, at Robinson May. Management decided they did not like my mini-skirts and put me in one of their latest fashions, a midi dress. Although beautiful in lavender with a cute jacket, I felt matronly in the long skirt down to my calves. Around this time the temp agency offered me a position working their front desk greeting clients and giving them tests for potential temp jobs. I really enjoyed it and became great lifelong friends with the owner and his family. This is when I advanced to the accounting department and learned how to do payroll. Larry located another job and life was bliss again. Soon we were able to take a little belated Honeymoon by going to Las Vegas for a few days. Larry bought me this cute pink drop waist short dress with pleats, and I wore white boots and a white floppy hat. My hair was long, and Larry loved the look! He always wanted me to dress kind of sexy, something he never stopped wanting me to do, even when I felt I was too old to do so. Wanting to please him I always tried to look my best. One day when Larry was walking to work, passing by Robinson May, he saw there was a career day in the lobby, so he went in to check it out. That is when he discovered the field of court reporting and the shortage of reporters there were at the time.

Las Vegas ~ 1970

Back to School

It was decided that Larry needed to go back to school and he decided the court reporting field was what he wanted to do. And since it was tied into the legal field, it seemed a good field to go into. The money was better than average and was a good thing for our family. But to accomplish this we needed to move in with his parents in their small house. We had a back bedroom for the four of us. We were grateful for their help and managed but with persistence we got through the two years he needed to complete the course. Turns out he was a natural for this line of work. He accomplished the 200 words per minute required to graduate and passed the state exam with flying colors and was hired by Santa Barbara Superior Court in Santa Barbara. It was off to the beautiful coastal town to look for a home and start a new life. We found a nice little house to rent and I got a job at a company that made microsurgical tools for surgery. I was hired for their accounting dept. There I met Suzie and we became friends for life and after meeting her significant other, the four of us took many trips together over the years.

Santa Barbara Superior Court ~ Our first House

Off to Santa Barbara

A bright new future was ours in this lovely town. We found a house to rent until we decided to buy. Not long after getting settled, we ran across an open house and fell in love with the home. It was a three-bedroom, large kitchen and good size living room and a nice back yard. This was around 1972 and the house was Thirty-three thousand nine hundred and fifty dollars. My parents helped us by giving us the down payment. The twins started school in that house, and all was going well. Then we decided a couple years later, to buy something a little larger as we planned to have more children around this time. We found a fixer upper not far from the beach and not far from our friends Suzie and John. The house was in bad condition. Black and silver wallpaper in the family room, and the carpet was so bad it fell apart when trying to remove it. They must have a lot of parties and spilled alcohol on it. It had been rented for many years. The owner decided to not deal with renters anymore and put it on the market. We did pay more for this one because of its location to the beach and it had 4 bedrooms, a separate large sunk in living room as well as a family room off the kitchen. We had it painted, new carpet, blinds, new appliances, and kitchen flooring. We had the kitchen cabinets stripped and stained as they were painted green. We also landscaped the front yard and painted the front of the house. Larry's father who was a carpenter by trade and made a beautiful front door with an oval glass inlay for us. We were pleased with everything and thought it looked so good. And it was so nice to be able to go down to the beach in 5 min. They had a food stand there, which many years later was turned into a nice restaurant with a patio for dining. During this time, we took several trips with our friends, introducing them to Palm Springs where they got married.

Our 2nd house up from the beach

A New Baby

As planned or maybe not, I became pregnant in the spring of 1976. Our little bundle of joy arrived on Oct. 22 and we were thrilled it was another girl. She had a head of dark wavy hair and Larry's beautiful green eyes. She looked like a little doll, so we named her Barbie. She grew up to look a lot like the first Barbie doll that was brunette and had green eyes. When she was around two, we took a trip down the delta on a houseboat with our friends. So much fun. The twins were athletic and were diving off the top of the houseboat and had a great time. Just one of the many trips we took with Suzie and John. One afternoon we went down to the beach and rented bicycles built for two and took a ride down the beach. Great fun and, of course, we made many more weekend trips to Palm Springs.

Barbie Lynn born Oct 22, 1976

Moving Again

After four years at the Santa Barbara Superior Court, things had become stressful for Larry. Murder cases were a bit much to continue to work on and proof, so he decided to check into freelance reporting for a private agency. The owner said there was a lot of work and he would be happy to have him on his team. He had a case he had to finish from the courts and that kept him busy for several months. He was then free to start with the new firm. It became apparent quickly that there really was not as much work as the owner stated. The income was high one month and extremely low the next. With a young family we could not manage this type of income. We needed to go to a larger city like Los Angeles or Sacramento. We did not want to go back to Los Angeles, so we chose Sacramento. Selling the house for double what we paid we thought we did good. (Many years later the property was worth 8 times that amount!!) So off we went up north to start a new life. We got a lovely two story, previously a model. It had beautiful landscaping and custom built-ins and drapes. Larry started with an agency in town and they kept him quite busy. I got a job in town as well and the three girls became active in the cabana club down the street, which had a diving team. The twins really loved it and did very well. Barbie joined the team when she was 5 and was able to swim across the deep end to qualify. All three girls were on the diving team in 1981 when our team competed against Davis. Our life currently was participating in judging the various diving events every weekend. This year our team won against Davis for the first time in 10 years. All three girls were a part of the team and channel 3 came out and filmed it. Little Barbie had done an impressive back dive. We were so proud of the them.

Holli

Heidi

Barbie

Trips with Friends

Our friends from Santa Barbara continued to meet us for different trips, no matter where we lived. One such trip, now that we were in Sacramento was a river rafting trip down the Sacramento River. Another was the trip down the Delta on a houseboat I mentioned earlier. Our friendship has spanned over 45 years, no matter where we moved to and we had certainly moved a lot by now. Many trips were made to Palm Springs. Always fun times with them. We were blissfully happy with our family and friends in our life. They had become like family, saw our children grow up and was part of their weddings and lives.

River rafting down the Sacramento
River with Suzie and John

Houseboat trip down the Delta
with friends Suzie and John

Another Baby

After settling into our new home in Sacramento, Larry was working regularly building up his income slowly, so I went back to work to help. In 1979 I found out I was pregnant giving birth to a large baby boy. Almost 10lbs. I was in labor for 10 hours. We were so happy to have a little boy this time. We named him Erik. Larry was so happy with his little family and the girls loved their little brother. It was about a year later we decided to sell the two story and buy a new single-story model being built around the corner. The two story just had become too much work. So, we moved again!

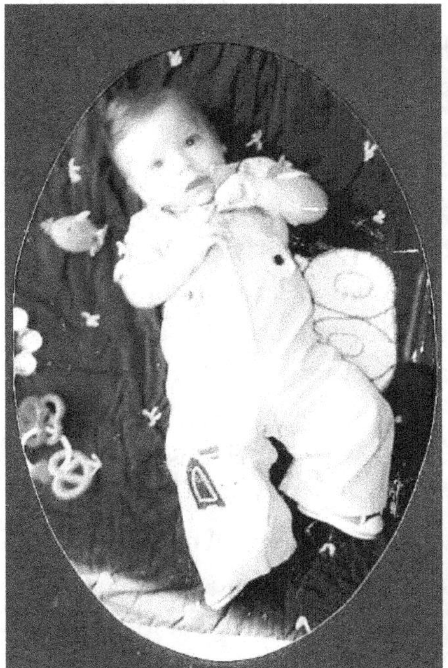

Erik Alan ~ born April 26, 1980

My favorite photo of Barbie and Erik on the giraffe at The Nut Tree

Multi-level Businesses

I was always looking for ways to earn extra money for the family and after many, many attempts over the years, I realized I missed out a lot with my children by being gone trying to "succeed" in various pyramid schemes. But I kept trying anyway.

I guess you could say my first try was with Avon, although not a pyramid scheme it was a home business. This is when I lived in the country and the twins were little. I found most ladies did not wear makeup and had little interest in the other products. My next try was as a Tupperware lady when we lived in Sacramento. I really, just wanted the kit of Tupperware out of it. Again, not terribly successful. After having had Erik I did start a daycare center and had 5 two year-olds that I ended up potty training and as soon as they were potty trained the mothers put them in day care and I had to start all over again with a new child. Really a lot of work! I then discovered a product called Mix-n-go, a gas additive for your car that gave you better gas mileage. This was a true pyramid scheme and after many trips out of town to Oakland for meetings, I lost interest. Larry was so supportive of all my businesses, and he was always there to take care of the kids and help with homework. And then there was Amway! You all have heard of that one I am sure. This one caused family and friends to be rather put out with me for trying to get them to join and or buy product. This did not last and ended up costing us money we did not have. After we moved to the single-story house in Sacramento, we had met a nice couple in the neighborhood who talked us into going to a meeting and low and behold it was Amway again! Sneaky of them but the speaker was so convincing we joined again! Turns out he and his wife had the meetings in their home and played a very impressive video on the television. Turns out they had twin girls, so we had a connection there. They had purchased $20,000 worth of product and had it stored in their garage and supplied there many distributors with product as they needed it. However, it turns out the wife got disenchanted with this business, files for a divorce and she and the girls ran off with an X-Amway distributor! Alas we saw many marriages ruined by these businesses, not just Amway. After getting out of that one and losing more money, another neighbor got us to come to a meeting at his house, again for circles on the wall!

This time it was a product called Meadow-fresh. A powdered milk product. Tasted good and the price to get in was right, so we signed up. But again, to succeed you had to sell product and recruit people, causing friends and family to get angry with us for asking. Oh, and by the way. this family was originally doing well, as the husband was in real estate and drove a Mercedes but ended up giving up his business for this one, with the circles on the wall, showing the supposed successes, but he ended up losing his car and his family of four children and another on the way, was living off-of peanut butter and jelly sandwiches and they lost the house as well. My advice…do not do any of them! It is a big waste of time, energy, and money not to mention being away from your family to work the business.

The Brass Business

Then I discovered my brother owned a Brass store in Arizona being run by my Aunt and Uncle. I took their catalogue and designed one of my own, pasting it over top of their catalogue and decided to start a Brass Party Plan. I had attended various parties and knew how they worked. So, I bought several pieces for wholesale and put them in a suitcase and started getting friends to have parties for me, giving the hostess a free piece of Brass for her trouble. Brass had become immensely popular at this time and my friends loved the unusual pieces I had. I was selling a lot and my brother took notice and wanted to help develop a team of consultants. So off I went recruiting ladies from my parties. He had put a kit together of the most popular pieces and the girls could pay for it through their sales. We also had a booth at the fairgrounds and recruited a couple who did very well with not only recruiting but with sales as well. We had 35 consultants the first year and $110,000 in sales. I became the leader so to speak, and would have meetings to keep the consultants excited, giving away prizes of beautiful brass piece for highest sales. For the Oakland group, I had to drive out once a month to keep that group motivated, since they were the largest group. My brother put on a seminar and gave out awards for top sales, like eel skin briefcases and larger pieces of brass. The consultants were all real excited. We even had a car outside showing how they could earn a car.

Unfortunately, shortly after that first year, the group that we sponsored at the fair, was arrested for welfare fraud, from stealing checks from people's mailboxes. Things went from bad to worse that next year. People were able to buy brass everywhere and for less. Sales suffered and consultants were having difficulty getting parties through their friends. We ended up losing all the consultants but one. At this point Brass had run its course and was no longer popular. Thus, another unsuccessful try at a business. But it did last longer than the others and I sure enjoyed it while it lasted and was grateful for my brother investing so much time, energy and money trying to make it a success. I know it cost him a lot. Another business I started after this was a Mylar Balloon business. These pretty shiny balloons had just come on the scene and were so pretty with unusual designs, I knew they would sell.

Who does not like balloons? I approached the toy store in the mall, and they allowed me to sell them in front of the store wearing my cute clown outfit I made. They received a % of the sales, but I did very well.

Then near Christmas I approached JCPenney to sell in front of their store and again they got a % of the sales. I wore a long plaid skirt with a white blouse and red vest with a Santa hat. Between the two stores and a few helpers we sold $8,000 dollars-worth of balloons. My last sale, or I should say give away was to a father who was walking by with his darling triplets. He could not afford to buy them all three a balloon and since it was Christmas Eve, I gave each little girl a balloon. They were thrilled and the father thanked me so much. Sure, wish I had gotten a picture of them. This was one of the more rewarding business's I started

Shortly after I had my balloon business, you could find the mylar balloons everywhere. The toy store got their own helium tank and sold balloons and you could find them out at the swap meets as well. But I was the first, at least in Sacramento at that time. This was 1980 not long after Erik was born. I was still nursing him, and Larry would bring him to the toy store, and I would take a break and go in the car to nurse him. He kept stopping and looking up at me wondering who I was with my clown makeup on. Poor kid, he was so confused

The Brass Business

My Balloon Business

Two Weddings and a Grandbaby

Our twins were graduating from high school and Holli announced she was getting married. So, we were now planning a wedding. She gave birth a couple years later to our first grandson David. It was a difficult six-year marriage and ended up in divorce. Heidi had also announced she was engaged to her longtime boyfriend but were not rushing into a marriage just yet.   It was at this time Larry discovered that the state was hiring court reporters and we needed to move back to Los Angeles. We had gotten

in debt during the 8 years in Sacramento because the agency he worked for did not take out taxes from his checks. He was considered an independent contractor. We just did not seem to be able to put money aside and ended up having a running bill with the IRS. We desperately needed a solid job that had benefits and the State of California was the answer. Larry took the state exam and passed, being hired by the State of California Workman's Comp Appeals Board in Santa Monica. A life saver for sure. It was at this time that Heidi who had broken up with her longtime boyfriend and had met Pat. The two took a trip to Japan to see his father who worked for the American Embassy there.

Holli gets married

Holli has our 1st grandchild ~ David

Upon returning from their trip they came to see us. Heidi says, "guess what this is?" as she unrolls a document all in Japanese. "Our marriage certificate"! They had gotten married while over there and Pats father gave them a trip around Japan as a wedding present. Quite an experience Heidi said. She said she made Pat promise to have a church wedding in the states before committing to marrying him in Japan. But because his parents could not come to the states for another year, they kept it a secret and had a lovely wedding a year later.

Holli reconnected with Kie, who she knew from Jr. High and who was also Asian. They fell madly in love and he loved her son. So, another wedding was planned. Amazing that the twins would both marry Asian men. They were always competitive that way! They did make beautiful children, six between them. Both girls were happy and that is all we cared about, not to mention they were both great son-in-law's!

Heidi and Pat Marry

A New Job for Larry

Finally, we were on solid footing with Larry's new job. We moved into a nice apartment with secure locked glass doors at the entrance. We felt safe again. And the elementary school was across the street for little Erik. However, it was not meant to be! There was a drug raid one day on our complex which was very scary. The police followed a van that had been stopping at our building and as it turned out one of the apartments was being used to store drugs. They pulled the two guys out of the van, making them lie down on the ground at gun point, feet spread and hands above their heads. They proceeded to try and get in the door but of course it was locked, yelling for someone to open the door before they broke the glass, someone did let them in and they rushed to the apartment not far from ours but about that time the guy in the apartment ran out the back and got away. That was it! We were moving again for sure. Too much danger here!

Turning 40

I could not believe I was turning the big four-O. I was just 17, wasn't I? The family gave me a nice party and the next day we drove down to join our friends Suzie and John for a birthday lunch. They were staying at the Del Coronado in San Diego.

Around this time our daughter Barbie and her cousin Diana took part in a performance of Annie, singing and dancing.   We were so proud of them both. Life was going well.

Barbie and cousin Diana
perform in "Annie"

My 40th Birthday

Disney - A sure thing...

Or so we thought! It was 1989 and another business idea came to us, only this time Larry was the inventor. He had designed a push toy, originally a cute duck and when you pushed it, the feet attached to the wheels came around and hit the arms that were hanging loose and it waddled and when the arms moved back and forth it made a noise. So cute. Eventually it evolved into Daisy and Donald Duck. I was able to get an appointment with the Disney Company in Burbank and they loved them. They suggested making Mickey, Minnie, Donald, and Daisy. They designed the decals and we found a manufacturer to produce them. The originals had a long stick, but Disney said to use a shorter stick for toddlers. So, we were off and running. They ordered $18,000 of the toys for both parks. However, it cost almost as much to make, so we did not make a profit on that order, but the Disney stores had ordered 10,000 toys. However, they cancelled soon after due to having too much inventory. Disappointed we thought we would sell them to toy stores outside the park but were stopped dead in our tracks when we found out Mattel had the rights to all Disney push and pull toys outside the park! We could not believe it. Another failed business, a very costly one as we borrowed the money from his parents to do this business. They had gotten a loan on their home and his stepdad had helped make the prototypes we presented to Disney in the first place. Disney never did order more. A crushing blow for sure. We almost made it!

The Prototypes

Our toys were put in Disneyland and the Disney World Park. This is the display window.

Another Move

Now that Larry was established in his State job and it was going well, our daughter was about to go into Jr. High, and we were concerned

about the LA schools and the bad elements there. We decided to check out the outlying areas and ended up settling on Valencia a beautiful little town up north. It would require us both to commute for our jobs but decided it was worth it. I was working for a CPA firm in West Los Angeles doing payroll and did like my job. So, we moved again! Valencia was a lovely town to raise a family in, so we were excited. I commuted for a while until I found a local job and stopped the commute to West LA. The kids seemed happy. Barbie graduated from Jr. High and Erik took up baseball for a short while. We were all there to cheer him on. Unfortunately, he wanted to quit because he was afraid of the ball. Our daughter Heidi graduated from Hancock College at this time as well. In October, our friends Suzie and John in Santa Barbara had a Halloween party we attended. We came as John Travolta and Olivia Newton John from Grease. We had a radio with us playing the music from the movie. They had a fun scavenger hunt around the neighborhood. A great party!

Heidi Graduates from
Hancock College

Barbie graduates Jr. High

34

A Fight, A Divorce and A Wedding

In 1992 Erik graduated from elementary school. During this time is when things fell apart for Holli. A serious fight occurred causing physical damage. She was rescued by her long- lost love from Jr. High who still had feelings for her. He would make UPS deliveries to the Hallmark store she worked for and they reconnected. Since she had been very unhappy in her marriage, she saw him as her savior. Kie was more than happy to take her son on as his. He was crazy about her. Thus, the fight and divorce followed. Kie and Holli were married in a beautiful ceremony in the Buddhist Temple on November 21, 1992. Both twins were married and happy.

Holli & Kie marry November 21, 1992 ~   Erik looks so happy here.

Winning!

April 1993 brought a wonderful surprise for Heidi and Pat. They were notified that Heidi had won the Mervin's One Hundred Thousand Dollar Mortgage Pay Off! Pat had put a coupon in the box for each of them when they last visited Mervin's, several months before, never dreaming they could win. But Heidi's name was picked out of 1.2 million people across the united states. They had recently purchased a home in Santa Maria and had paid a little over that for the home. Mervyns in fact paid off their mortgage and they were free and clear of any house payments. This opportunity allowed Heidi to finish her education. As well as the ability to do a little traveling during the school breaks. They were on TV and a poster was made of Heidi and the store manager of the Santa Maria store and was put in all the stores across the United States. She was now a celebrity!

More Outings & Another Wedding

During this new year of 1994 I had my 20 Year reunion and time to reconnect with old classmates and see what everyone had been doing. There were several pool parties at our friends in Santa Barbara. The girls and their husbands came down as well. It was great having everyone together. Our daughter Barbie turned 18 and we gave her a surprise limo ride where she stopped to pick up a couple of friends and her boyfriend at the time, stopping

to get some lottery tickets since she was legal to buy them, then proceeded to go to the dealership I currently worked for, surprising her with a new little car. We had balloons attached and a Happy Birthday sign on the windshield. She was thrilled to say the least.

We then received a wedding invitation from the GM of the dealership that was done up on a cowboy boot and was being held at the old movie set out in the hills. It was an old western town used for the movies a long time ago. In the small wooden church, there were bales of hay we sat on. The bride wore a white cowboy hat with her white dress and groom wore a black cowboy hat with his black tux.

After the ceremony we walked down towards the saloon with swinging doors, but before we got there, they had a pretend fight over the bride in the middle of the dirt road, using blanks in their guns. It was really something. We then went into the saloon and on into the room where the reception was. The tables were set up with tin plates and red kerchief napkins. So original in how they did everything. They had great music to dance to and all the drinks you wanted. We all dressed in western outfits as well. So much fun. One wedding we will always remember.

Barbie gets a car

My boss's amazing wedding

A fun pool party at friends Suzie & Johns

Graduation and an Anniversary Party

In 1995 Barbie graduated from High School and at the same time Heidi graduated from college with her master's degree. So proud of them both. This year marked our 25th Wedding Anniversary and we just had to have a party. We decided to have it at the Be Bop Café on State street in Santa Barbara. I came as a cheerleader and Larry found a letterman's coat at a second-hand store and came as a football player. The café had special parking spots named after stars and of course we got the Elvis spot since I was a big fan. Inside they had a movie marque and they put the name "A Summer Place with Troy Donahue and Sandra Dee' commemorating our song from the movie. We had pink and white balloons hanging from the ceiling and I had made these cute place mats in the shape of 45 records with names of the different songs we liked. We invited family and special friends we had known for years. Our friends Suzie and John came, and we asked John to do a mock wedding. I brought a vail to put on and John came as a pastor. Suzie was a hippie flower child. John had the cutest speech for us, I wish I had kept a copy of the script he wrote. It was so funny. Larry had bought me a new ring, so we did exchange rings. I still wore my original ring that we had made, using my old diamonds from my first marriage. That always bothered him, but we could not afford a whole new ring at the time. Suzie and John took us to a really nice place for dinner after the party. We stayed at a local hotel on the beach and the girls got in and decorated the room and the hotel gave us a bottle of champagne, wishing us Happy Anniversary. A very memorable Anniversary. The Be Bop Café has since been torn down and is now just a parking lot. Nothing ever stays the same it seems.

Carousel of Dreams ~ Fleischer

Barbie and Heidi graduate

Our 25th Anniversary party

Family Life

By this time Erik had gotten taller than Larry who was 6'1" tall. (Erik ended up being 6'5" tall) I have no idea who that came from since both grandfathers were 5'8" tall. And I think Larry's great grandfather was four foot something! Barbie moves out with a girlfriend and learns about finances and paying rent. Erik got his first job with Wendy's. We made a few more trips this year with our friends, one being a trip to Laguna Beach, quickly becoming our favorite place over Palm Springs. One trip was to have dinner at The Patio restaurant and to see the Pageant of The Masters show. It is a wonderful renactment of the old masters and their paintings. The people were painted in such a way that when they took their places on stage and a large frame came into place, it looked just like the real painting. It was truly, amazing. Another outing was to see the movie "Singing in the Rain" and dinner afterwards. Always memorable fun times. Erik was turning 16 and enjoying skateboarding and video games with his friends. It was the calm before the storm I feared.

Barbie new apartment ~ Eriks favorite sport-skate boarding

A family photo in Santa Barbara

Twins and more Twins

Hollie and Kie were happy and doing well. Holli decided to get further education, going back to school and became an MA, getting a job at Kaiser medical facility. We were so proud of her. In 1997 we made a trip to Arizona to see mom in the Ms. Senior beauty Pageant. All her 7 sisters and brothers came as well as the twins and their husbands and my brother. There was a party after the pageant for mom's 70th birthday. She did not win but looked beautiful in her black sequin gown. She sang a moving song as her talent but lacked the speaking ability like the one who took home the crown. I admire her for trying this at this time of her life.

During this time Holli and Kie announced they were pregnant and soon after called me at work one day saying "Are you sitting down? There's two!" They were having twins! I could not believe it. Everyone was so excited. On July 9th Kimiko (Kimi for short) and Takato (T.J. for short) where born. Two little bundles of joy for sure. Then – wait for it! Heidi and Pat announced they were having twins! Christian and Brandon were born on March 16th, eight months after Holli and Kie's twins. Four grandchildren in one year. What a blessing!

Holli graduates as a medical assistant. So proud of her.

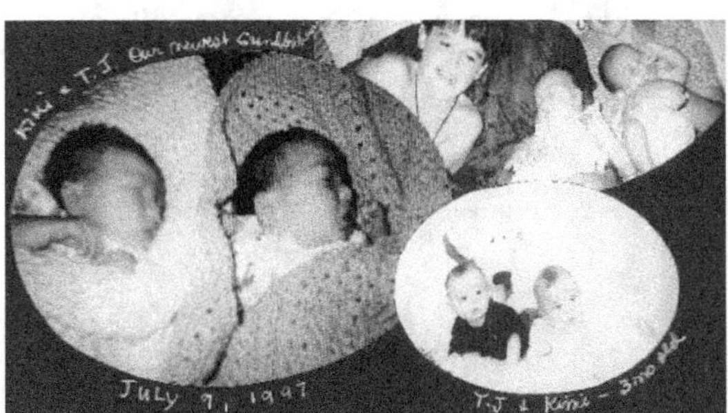

Kimi and T.J.~ Holli & Kies twins

Christian & Brandon ~ Heidi & Pats twins

Erik's Struggles.

It was November 1997 when our son came to me and said he felt something was wrong and he needed to see a doctor. Being only 17 he had to see a pediatrician. Here is this kid who is 6'5" tall in the waiting room of a children's Doctors office. He was desperate it seemed. And wanted to go in to see the doctor by himself. We got a referral for a psychiatrist who we made an appointment right away. The doctor diagnosed Erik~with having schizophrenia. It could not be! This tall good-looking kid with so much potential. He was unbelievably artistic, drawing detailed pictures of skateboarders, his favorite subject.

Erik Graduates ~ 1998

Erik off to his first job at Windys

A surprise for Erik

The doctor put him on Paxil and referred him to a counselor. He turned 18 in April and was becoming more and more panicked.

He would call me to come pick him up from school because he could not seem to go into the classroom. Because of his diagnosis we were able to get him home schooling for a few months. He did not like the way the Paxil made him feel and refused to take it. He returned to school the last few weeks and did graduate with his class. Still struggling, our niece came out to help by just being there for him to talk to. We both had to work. She stayed with us for three months driving back and forth to her job in Los Angeles at night and then spend the days listening to Erik. I will be forever grateful to her for this selfless act. It was what he needed, to be able to talk to someone daily. Something we could not provide for him.

We felt we needed to give Erik the same gift as our daughter Barbie, hoping this would somehow make a difference. So, for his 18th birthday we had a limo take him to pick up a couple of friends, stop and get a few lotto tickets, driving on to the dealership I worked for. There we had a black truck with balloons and a sign saying Happy Birthday. He was thrilled of course. Both Barbie and Erik were expected to get jobs to help pay for the cost of their own cars. At this time, we moved again to a condo we were trying to buy. Erik was working at Wendy's and Barbie was working at the dealership with me in the rental department. Things were looking up.

Suicide Note

Erik became more and more withdrawn and one day I came home from work and found a suicide note and some cash on the table. I panicked and got in the car to go look for him. I realized that he was on his skateboard and would be on the paseos running between the homes and I would never see him. I returned home not knowing what to do next. Entering the apartment, I saw him sitting on the patio with a blank expression on his face. Running up to him hugging him he was stiff and unfeeling. I saw that he tried to cut his wrist. I was beside myself. We took him to a different counselor hoping this would make a difference. Erik was still depressed but did not want to take medication. Being 18 we could not force him to do so. He could not understand why he felt the way he did. He was given antianxiety medication by the new doctor, but he just did not like to take them because it made him feel numb.

Erik in happier times

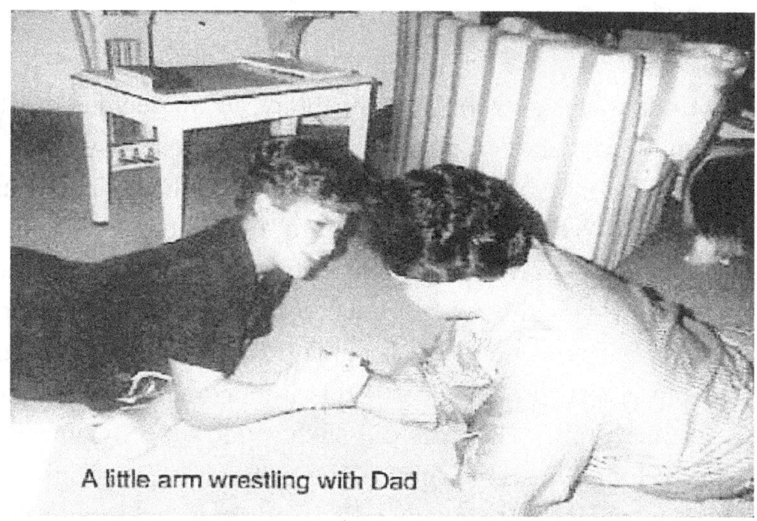

A little arm wrestling with Dad

Family Events

It was our daughter's twenty-first birthday, so we decided to take the family to a magic dinner show club in Universal Studios. It was so much fun, and everyone seems to have a good time including Erik. This was also the year I turned 50! Where did the years go??   All the kids and Larry planned a surprise party. Larry took me to a beautiful brunch and when we came back everyone was inside when I opened the door. Friends from high school, from Santa Barbara and the girls came down from Sacramento with the babies and biggest surprise was an Elvis impersonator! He sang like Elvis. It was so much fun. The girls did such a good job of putting it all together. A party I shall never forget.   The following Thanksgiving, we traveled to Las Vegas where my cousin who lived there had invited us all to come for the Thanksgiving festivities. It was quite a reunion with her husband and four boys, all grown. My sister and two of her boys were in town for a baseball tournament and came. Erik got to meet some of his cousins and seemed to enjoy himself. Mom and dad flew in as well. Then Christmas was just around the corner and was being held at Holli and Kies this year. Enjoying the two sets of twins, we had a very, nice Holiday. I believe Mom and dad came up as well. In 1999 Erik turned 19 and wanted to go miniature golfing. The four of us enjoyed the day and we were hoping Erik was doing ok, but we were were never sure from day to day.   Another family get together occurred at my brother's daughter's graduation from college in San Diego.   We all drove down for the ceremony and dinner afterwards except Erik. He refused to go. All four of my brother's girls were there so Barbie got a chance to meet her cousins. We had not seen much of them since my brother and their mother divorced many years ago and he had remarried and had another daughter, who had come along. Another great reunion.

Living in Valencia at the time, my sister later that year, came out from Texas, camping along the way, bringing mom with her. We all went to Magic Mountain and had a great time. I was sorry to see them go. An outing with Heidi, Pat and the twins was made in August, having a picnic on the lawn of the Hollywood Bowl, and enjoying a performance afterwards. The babies were so good. Rounding out the summer was another pool party at Suzie and Johns for the 4th of July. To end the summer was a trip to Laguna Beach for another Festival of the Arts with mom and her new friend. Mom and Dad had divorced by this time.

Erik

Erik was working and seemed to be doing ok at this time. Daughter Barbie is surprised one day by her x-boyfriend on her 23rd birthday and does not tell her where they are going or us for that matter. He took her to go skydiving. She was terrified but consented to do it since he had paid for it and she would be jumping with an instructor. The pictures show her coming down and landing. She said it was thrilling but she would never do it again! Christmas was at Holli and Kies and mom flew in as well. All the twins were growing and getting so cute. On New Year's Day, we took Erik and went to see The Queen Mary. It was a nice day and Erik seemed to enjoy it. In 2000 Heidi and Pat had a little girl who they named Kira. Larry was so fond of her. He was there when she took her first steps toward him. They kept this bond for life.

Erik was still struggling and changed jobs frequently. He had started college but dropped out because he simply could not concentrate. He had a hard time relating to his fellow coworkers as well as the customers. He always seemed up tight and seldom smiled. At this time, he joined a church, making a few close friends. Still searching for an answer to what he was going through. He had met a fellow name Josh who ended up living with us a few months and was a big help to Erik. They stayed friends a long time and he is close to our family still. Another one of his friends asked if he wanted to drive cross-country with him to Camp Red Cloud in the Colorado mountains.   He hesitated but decided he would go.   The two became camp counselors for the kids there.   We were so surprised he would go, and we were pleased he would take this opportunity.   He really struggled but made it through the three-month commitment.   During this time, he met a guy with the church named Chrisjon, who took him under his wing and spent a lot of time with Erik.

While Erik was in Colorado, he felt the need to talk to him, but he was over in Egypt on a mission. I gave Erik a calling card to use and he tried to call Egypt, but it was $53 min! So, he could not talk long. But whatever he needed was ok with us.

Erik and friend are off to Colorado ~ Camp Red
Cloud to be counselors.

A skydiving experience Barbie
will never forget.

A day visiting the Queen Mary

The Arrest

After Erik returned from his trip and his friend returned from his mission overseas, the two spent a lot of time together. Erik was still searching for answers and went to many of the upper parishioners in the church and could only get the answer "pray about it". He eventually concluded that there was no room in the church for mental illness. They simply did not have any real answers on what to do. And the medical society's answer was pills. One day Erik was supposed to meet his friend for dinner and never showed up. His friend came over to the house looking for Erik. Just before he arrived, two officers came to our door asking for Erik.   He was wanted for stealing a gun from a pawn shop in town. I became hysterical because I knew what he wanted to do. He was not home, and we did not know where he was. His friend called other members of the church and they came over with food and offered to help look for him. We did not know where to even start but I knew he had a credit card and called the company and explained the situation and they were so helpful. He had driven out to Green Valley to a shop to buy bullets. After that we did not know where he went. He could be anywhere. All we could do was wait and hope he contacted us. Two days later he called at five am in the morning saying simply "Mom, go to the computer and look up Dr. Kevorkian". Relieved to hear his voice, I said "Erik he only helps terminally ill people and he is probably in jail anyway." He says to me "but I am terminally ill." Erik's friend, Chrisjon had stayed with us and heard the call, so I turned the phone over to him to try and talk Erik into turning himself in.   He just did not realize how much trouble he was in. It does not matter if you stole the gun to harm yourself and not others, it is a serious crime! My heart was broken to think of my son in jail. It took many hours for Erik to tell his friend where he was and to agree to turn himself in. He finally agreed and his friend found him at the top of the hill in the Taco Bell parking lot, out of gas and money. The gun was in the back seat with Larry's prop gun from his collection that Erik took. Apparently using it to convince the lady to turn over the gun that he had looked at earlier. The owner was in the back. Erik ran out the door, the owner running after him.

He had his daily organizer with him and threw it at the man to slow him down (with all his contact information inside!). He jumped in the car and took off but not before the owner kicked in the driver's window shattering it. Apparently, Erik had been inside to look at a gun and left when he found out you had to wait 10 days before taking possession.

He simply could not wait! He sat in the car for a while deciding what to do. Of course, he had this planned since he had taken his dads prop gun. He could not go through with the shooting himself and shot up in the air instead.   His friend Chrisjon took him to the police station, and he turned himself in. A parent's worst nightmare come true. He was taken to the Los Angeles jail downtown. The first time we were able to see him, it was devastating. The waiting room was a very cold place, packed with people waiting to see their loved ones. All of us in the same boat, different circumstances.

We rode up in the elevator and walked down to the window where he stood in his orange jump suit putting his hand up to the window and I matching his on the other side with tears running down my cheeks. (This is so hard to write about. Brings back the pain all over again, like it was yesterday. Yet, it has been 15 years ago. You never get over something like this).

He said to me the instant I picked up the phone was "Mom, I'm not going to make it in here." I know he believed that, but we knew that his condition was not terminal. We tried to comfort him and told him we would be getting an attorney and get him out as soon as possible, not knowing for sure how long he would be sentenced to. Our hope was knowing his condition and he was only trying to hurt himself, that the courts would be lenient. Where had we gone wrong, that he would resort to stealing a gun to kill himself? We tried to help him, but nothing seemed to work. He just did not see a way out of his overwhelming condition.

Probation

We now had to look for an Attorney and were not sure where to look. Through the church we were recommended a good one, however they wanted six thousand dollars, which we did not have. So, we started a GOFUNDME, which saved us. Friends, family, and strangers donated what we needed. I will forever be grateful to everyone who helped us. Erik was a good kid, not a criminal and he was so desperate to end his life, that he did not know what else to do. We were fortunate to have a woman judge who felt compassion for Erik and saw that each day we had lots of family and friends who came to be with us in the courtroom to support us and Erik. He was given three years in county jail. I guess it could have been worse. Three years did seem a long time thought. However, one morning we got a call at 5am from Erik, five months later, that he was let out and he was waiting out front. I could not believe he was let out at five am in the morning on the dangerous streets of Los Angeles! We drove down as quickly as possible and there he was standing there all alone in his jeans and t-shirt, all 6' 5" of him looking so sad. Since he celebrated his birthday in jail, we wanted to invite his friends from the church over. but he really did not want to see anyone. He was put on probation for the rest of his time due and was required to report to a probation officer once a month in Los Angeles. He was also to see a doctor and take medication and start counseling again. After a few trips down to report to the probation officer, he called me and said he could see how Erik was struggling to even go in the door to report with the others. He just could not be around the other paroles. The very-nice officer said he could just call in once a month. What a break. He was lucky with a nice judge and probation officer as well.

Abby

I am questioning why now I decided to write my story, as I cannot help but cry about that sad time in our lives. I guess because there is a story to be told and it may help others who may have gone through something similar, knowing they are not alone in this type of struggle.

Barbie and I thought we would come up with something we thought would make Erik happy. He had wanted a dog for so long. So, we found an adorable puppy to adopt at Pet Co. We put her in a wrapped box and put a red bow around her neck. She was 6 weeks old and all black. Erik had no idea. When he saw the box, he thought it might be a kitten. When he opened the lid and this little black head popped up jumping up and down to get out, he had the biggest smile on his face. He lifted her up cuddling her. We knew this is what he needed. There is nothing better than to have a little dog to love and care for. It was emotional support for him. Hopefully, this would help.

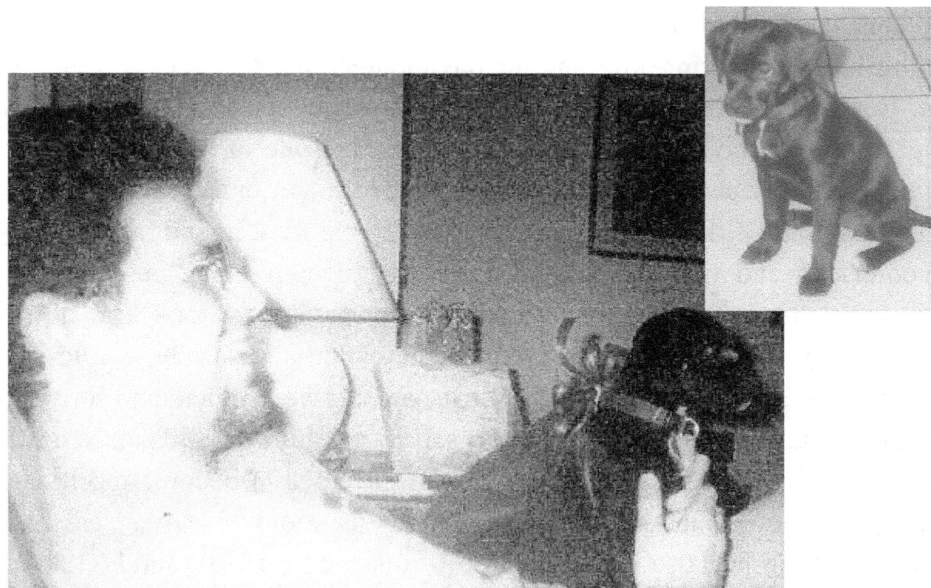

A puppy for Erik ~ he named her Abby

Moving Again

We were renting a cute house in the bungalows in Valencia at this time and had the opportunity to buy an older home in Canyon Country. In those days, the creative financing that was available, since we did not have a down payment, was a 1st and a 2nd for the down payment, meaning 100% financing. Big mistake! We loved the house even though we thought the price was a little high for our budget. Somehow, we were convinced we could afford it. It looked like a colonial style house with a large oak tree off to the right, shading the house. The backyard was marvelous with palm trees and a lovely kidney shaped pool. The pool sold the house for sure! I needed a little paint and carpet is all. It also had 5 bedrooms. Two of which were a Jack and Jill where the wall was removed to make one big room.

This was 2003 and Erik was still required to meet with a counselor and take medication. He was becoming more and more anxious about the meetings and refused to go into the waiting room with the others and wanted to stay in the car until the last patient was seen and then he would go in. This doctor changed his medications several times, trying to find one that worked. Nothing really seemed to help. He started getting bloated looking after taking the medications for over a year by this time. We talked to our insurance company to see if they had a program that he could be a part of and there was one in the valley. Erik did not want any part of it but finally he agreed to get in the car. Arriving at the facility he did not want to go in. Finally, he went in and he talked to the counselor and as usual, Erik has this way of convincing people there is no problem, so they excepted him as a day patient. I took him down the next day and dropped him off, but he called and said he would not stay there as he felt out of place. Most patients were older than he was. Back to ground zero again. I was so sad to see him lose his handsome looks from the medications he was on. He seemed to become more and more agoraphobic and hardly came out of his room by now. He had stopped driving because his perception of distance was off, and he felt he might have an accident. Barbie moved home again and was there to keep him company.

Brother and Sister

Our home in Canyon Country

Another New Puppy

2004 proved to be an interesting year. Along with Erik's constant struggles our daughter saw nine puppies on the front lawn of a near-by neighbor and  witnessed the pound picking them all up, taking them to their facility. She decided right then  and there she had to rescue them, all of them! Driving down to the pound she gave them $200 to pick all of them up.   She and a friend went around the neighborhood and found homes for them all but kept the little white one with the black ears and a black spot on her back and tail and the most beautiful crystal blue eyes ever.   Her sisters and brothers were all black and brown. Amazing! We now had a new member of the family. She was named Bella for beautiful. Erik fell in love with her as well. Now Abby had a companion. Barbie taught her to swim. She loved the water. Abby did not want any part of the pool. Bella unfortunately was the instigator in causing trouble, like chewing a hole in the bottom of the fence and running around the neighborhood with Abby hot on her trail. We had to replace the fence and Erik helped me paint it.   Fortunately, someone saw them and called me. It had rained their paws were muddy and we had just gotten a new car with cream interior. I was so mad at those two!

Painting the new fence

Teaching Bella to swim

A Graduation and Losing a Parent

In June, our first grandson David graduated from High School. Then in December we got a call that Larry's dad was in the hospital in Ferndale, way up north.   That is seven hours above Sacramento. The only fast way to get there was by plane, so off we went. Unfortunately, he passed when we were in the air. Larry was so very, sad since they had not been close over recent years and even

Grandson David Graduates

while growing up since his parents had divorced when he was six. Leonard was quite the character on his motorcycle. Larry nearly had a heart attack when he took 5-year-old Barbie for a ride sitting in front of him. Larry stayed up all night writing a eulogy for the service. His Aunt Trudy, Leonard's sister lived in town and still got around very well, even though she was 90. She said she would be there, along with a lady friend of Leonard's and other people in the tiny community. Our daughter Holli and Kie drove up as well and helped with clearing out his apartment. Larry's speech was heartfelt. Leonard always complimented me, and he was forever a fan of me as the girl for Larry.

Leonard on his motorcycle

Larry's Dad

Suicidal

Erik had stopped going to a therapist all together, refused to get out of the car at the last session. He said it was not helping him at all. I tried talking to him, asking him what was going on inside his head. He said the images I see are so terrifying you would not believe it. He said repeatedly that he was not going to live to be 40 or 50 with this condition. That we should throw him in the pool and let him drown. He then started talking about Denmark and Euthanasia that they do there for people who want to die. He sat at the table while I called and fortunately got ahold of a very nice lady who explained in fairly good English, that you had to be a resident for 6 months and then the courts had to approve after a doctor declared you were terminal, all of which I explained to Erik as he sat their listening to my conversation. He was dead serious.   My heart went out to him. He just wanted the suffering to stop. One night we became concerned with how he was talking and felt we needed to call 911. Five paramedics came in and forced him into the ambulance. All the while he is yellowing "Mom you shouldn't have done this." We followed in our car and waited for several hours for a doctor to come around. She came finally and concluded Erik was at that moment not suicidal. As usual, he had her convinced he was not going to do anything. So, they would not keep him the 72 hours hold. We then contacted a gentleman in Culver City who might be able to help. He drove up and spent two hours in Erik's room talking to him since Erik refused to come down. Afterwards he came down and we talked on the front lawn and he said he thought what he could do was send someone up a couple times a week to befriend Erik and try to get him out of his room to go do things together. However, before we could implement the plan, Erik took matters into his own hands.

He's Gone

Our daughter had gone to a friend's briefly, returning and looking for Erik. She called in a panic asking where Erik was. I said, "he's got to be there, he doesn't have a car." In the next instant she let out a scream, dropping the phone. My coworker heard the conversation and offered to drive me home. Pulling up to the house, there was a fire truck and police cars. I jumped out running into the house. An officer was blocking my path out to the garage. Barbie was on the floor doubled over crying hysterically. I kneeled-down hugging her and crying as I knew he was gone. My friend asked her pastor to come over to help the family get through this difficult time. She also was so kind to make the phone calls that needed to be made. Larry was waiting at a therapist office that I was to bring Erik later to meet him for a new session. My friend offered to come pick Larry up and drive him home, but he said he could drive. He arrived half an hour later. I ran to him and we hugged and cried. The people investigating brought us a note and Erik's glasses that he had in his pocket. It said, "He saw no other way out of the agony he was in. That he loved us, and we had to get through this." It was June 28, 2005. He had chosen to hang himself in the garage when Barbie found him. The operator said she had to cut him down in case he was still alive. I felt so bad for her having to find him and do that. Alas it was not to be, he was gone forever. My beautiful son, my baby was gone. This is so hard to write. It brings that painful day back so vividly I can hardly bear it. Losing a child is the most unbearable thing you can imagine.

The Memorial

The next few days were a blur of having to make funeral arrangements, picking a casket, purchasing a plot, ordering flowers, and notifying family. I could not bear to have an open casket. We did not want that to be our last image of our son. We had a graveside service and only close family and friends were invited. My brother came out from back east representing the family. Everyone had arrived and as we approached the group, I saw my brother and we hugged, crying together for our loss. Larry had written a beautiful poem that, after the pastor spoke, he read aloud. We played the song from the movie "Finding Private Ryan." Sad music but very moving and appropriate for the mood at this very-sad time. I cannot listen to it today as it brings back too many sad feelings of that day. Our girls and their families came down from Sacramento and Simi Valley to be with us. They too were saddened in losing their only brother. One who they loved and cherished all his life. Heidi's doctor did not recommend making the 4 ½ hour trip since she was due to deliver her 4th baby in two weeks! But said she did not care if she had the baby on the way down or at our place, she had to be there for her brother. We had a reception at the house and Lexus, who I worked for at the time, provided the food for our guests. My brother gave us a gift of money to get away for a few days. We were so grateful as we really needed that time to deal with our loss. Heidi and Pat returned to Sacramento and a week later Landun was born. Close call!

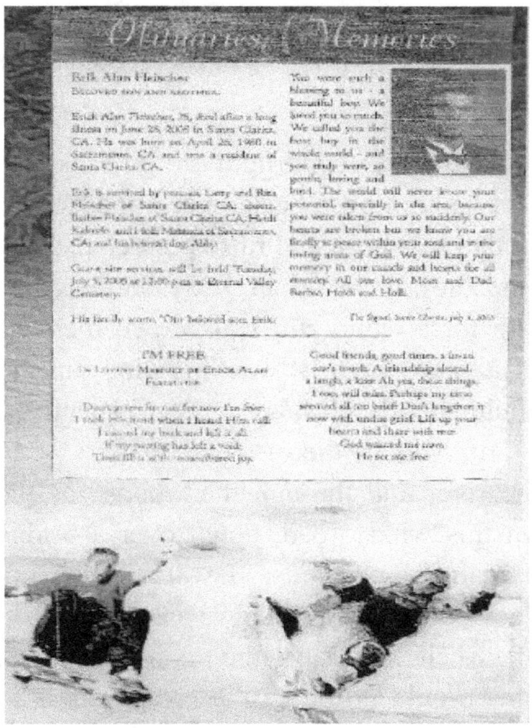

A Trip to Pennsylvania

Around September 2005 I was given an opportunity to go back east to Pennsylvania where I was born. I had not been back since 1965 when I was 17 for the Cassel reunion. My dad was born and raised there, the last of eight children born in the home they grew up in. My brother flew my parents there and we all met up for a wonderful walk down memory lane. We would go back every year when I was growing up, to celebrate Thanksgiving and my grandparent's birthdays. Consequently, I grew up with all my cousins, of which there were many. My grandparent's home was "Over the river and through the woods" as the song goes. You would drive down this windy road, down over a bridge and the two-story house set back against the woods. I walked with my grandfather and his dog into those woods every time we came to visit. I have such fond memories of when at 5am the coo-coo clock would go off and my grandmother would go down the creaky stairs to collect the wood for the stove and start breakfast. She made the best pancakes on that wood burning stove. There was always M&Ms, pretzel stick and Lebanon bologna in the center of the round claw foot table to snack on all day. One year when we all gathered at the house, all the cousins decided to go explore the forest. As we all spread out, we suddenly heard my cousin yell "yellow Jackets!" We all scattered. One got on my sock, but I pulled the material away from my skin avoiding getting stung.   My brother and Sammy, who had apparently stepped on a nest, got stung all over their backs and chest.   I remember grandma applying baking soda to their stings to draw out the poison. Never did that again! Our trip included the Hershey factory, which had been turned into an amusement park and gift shop.   And we did see some Amish buggies on the road in our travels.   The best part was the new owners of my grandparent's house was happy for us to come in and look at the house where dad grew up. The old wood burning stove was gone and had been modernizes and in-door plumbing had been added, there for no more out house that my grandmother insisted on using even when the indoor plumbing was added. I had one day left and my cousin Doris asked if I wanted to go to New York. I said is it that close and she said yes, she goes all the time. So we went, toured the city ending the day with New York Cheesecake in Ghirardelli Square. A trip I shall never forget.

Over the River and through The Woods....
FRANK • LUTHER • JOHN • PAUL
VIOLA • FANNY • JULIE
MARTIN + DAISEY
To grandmothers House we go.
The Cassel Home
TAKEN IN THE 50's
Memories

Summer 2005
TOUR
HERSHEY'S
CHOCOLATE WORLD

Another Move

I still have Erik's dresser filled with all his possessions. His bible with all the numerous notes on the side lines of each page. He tried so hard to find the answer to what was wrong with him. We miss him so much every day. I often wonder what type of a man he would have become and if he would marry and have a family. I think he wanted those things but saw no way to accomplish it in his condition. It has been 15 years and I cannot bear to let go of his dresser. There are still so many questions. Why was he struck down in the prime of his life with this awful disease? All the doctors and therapists he had could not seem to help. The only answer was drugs of which when he finally was forced to take, made him lethargic and unmotivated and he himself did not want to live that way the rest of his life. He said to me he was so lonely. That this condition isolated him from his friends and people in general. He could not work or socialize or even try to go to school or have a normal life. He could not concentrate or be in a classroom situation. I often wished there were a magic pill to make him all better but there is no such thing. I think most who have Schizophrenia end up committing suicide because they cannot live with it. Erik tried two times before succeeding on the third. Sometimes I think losing a child to an accident would be better than dealing with a disease that you have no control over and that doctors don't know how to treat, feeling helpless to help your child, to make it better. (hear I go again, starting to cry. This is so very, hard to relive)They say you should not make any moves during a time like this but we had been struggling financially with this house and the costs to hang on to it, that we decided to put the house on the market because we knew it would take some time to sell. Also, you were required to divulge that someone died in the house, which might make it undesirable to purchase for superstitious reasons. However, we did sell, closing escrow in June, the one-year anniversary of losing our son. We could now move on, keeping him in our hearts forever. We joined a group called "Compassionate Friends" that was an organization for parents who have lost a child of any age. The meetings helped us realize we were not a lone and really helped us with our loss.

They would meet once a month and had an annual picnic where we would stand in a circle, each saying this is for my son, or daughter and we had notes attached to a helium balloon, all letting them go at the end.

Seeing those balloons go up in the air, all the colors against the blue sky, gave us hope our loved one would get our messages. Then every December we met the 1st Sunday of the month to read poems, of which Larry wrote two for the group, sang and celebrated our children's lives, however short or long they were. They added a slide show last time we were there, showing pictures of each child. At 7pm we all had candles and lit them together and this was done in every city all around the world. It was such a special way to remember our children. The house being sold and not getting much out of it due to a couple of refinancing's, we decided to move to a 55+ apartment complex until we decided where we wanted to retire to.

Larry's Poems

During the next couple of years after losing our son, my husband started writing poems about our son and the pain of losing a child. It was his way of coping with this loss. They were so moving and beautiful. At this time, I had discovered creating books on-line for my grandchildren whenever they had a birthday party. I would put the photos on pages creating a book for them to remember there special day. These were nice because I could give them as gifts. Over time Larry had written quite a few poems. One day he had come up with a title and was working on the poem when I saw that the title was "Carousel of Dreams." I immediately knew which picture should go with that poem. I was quite surprised when I found the photo I was looking for since we had moved so many times by this time. The photo was of Erik on a Carousel at age 5, waving to the camera. This then became the cover for the special book I created with all of Larry's beautiful poems.

These are the poems Larry wrote about our son and our unimaginable loss:

Erik age 5 in 1985

Carousel of Dreams

Round and round, the world turns with tears,
Like a carousel swirling with shattered mirrors,
Memories keep changing with glittering murals,
Paintings on a merry-go-round that forever whirls.

Round and round, the years prance by
Like jewel-laden ponies that dance in the sky
A little boy's life filled with laughter and fun,
His future still beckoning and not yet begun.

Round and round, the heart prays anew,
Protect my child so his dreams will come true.
While leopards and lions rise and fall,
Watch over my boy until he is strong and tall.

Round and round, the years spin on,
A young man stands before me, his childhood gone.
No more the carousel, with memories so dear,
Zebras and tigers no longer appear.

Round and round, the lights start to dim,
The bells and the music have stopped for him.
He has been taken from me, my beautiful boy,
The world seems to hold less feelings of joy.

Round and round, magical steeds move by,
Memories play like a lost lullaby.
My soul has come to know the heartache within,
Haunted by thoughts of what might have been.

Round and round, the kaleidoscope turns,
He's now gone forever, but my heart still yearns.
For the carousel of dreams repeats eternally,
With his whisper over time, "remember me."

Erik's Senior picture ~ 1998

Beloved Son

A young man lies here, beautiful and serene.
His love so pure and dear; his sacrifice supreme.
His mother and his father thrilled, with his birth and life.
Praying all things be fulfilled, without struggle or strife.

His face was fair, a blessed one, a golden boy was he.
But destiny called to take our son, our dreams were not to be.
For him, this cruel and heartless end, never a spark of hate,
His character and majesty transcend this strange and tragic fate.

For he possessed a courage rare to fight his ills so deadly,
Strength was his beyond compare, his faith and love so steady.
He lost his battle in the end, his family pained and shattered.
But hope is his for us to mend, the lives left torn and tattered.

He wants us to know he is free, the dark years finally released.
His fervent prayer is for us to see, his heart is home, his soul at peace.
Hold him there, embraced in time, safe and without a care,
A sacred image in our mind, triumphant over all despair.

As eternity calls, we lift-up our eyes, to a vision beyond life and death,
Though heaven may fall and worlds collide, as long as we may have breath
We shall remember; we shall abide, with our love as vast as the ocean.
Though your life be undone, O' beloved son, eternal will be our devotion.

When Shadows Fall

When shadows fall across the land
I come to this mournful place,
With quiet thoughts of my beloved son
And visions of his youthful face.

The trees shimmer in the wind
And clouds grow dark and gray,
A misty rain falls from on high,
My troubled heart begins to pray.

Why did his future follow this fate?
How could it possibly be?
The mind struggles for answers to know,
Questions that will echo for eternity.

Now at his graveside, I come to find peace,
Standing in the cold March air,
Yearning for comfort and meaning here,
Fighting the feelings of hopeless despair.

The flowers left last on his gravestone
Have lost hope and finally died.
Their withered petals blow in the wind, while
my soul starts to struggle inside.

I lift-up my eyes to the heavens,
A scream in my mind cries out,
Thunder ripples across the sky,
Bringing waves of failure and doubt.

At last the storm passes over,
Tears of rebirth have begun.
Twilight sparkles through clouds overhead,
Love joins us - father and son.

Anthem for Lost Youth

Where are the children, the lost souls of youth?
The love of our lives gone by.
Our search is eternal, when taken from us,
So deep in our hearts they lie.

The infant toddler just learning to walk,
With unsteady steps so few,
The helpless hand now reaching in trust,
The eyes full of joy for you.

The mastery of concepts and reading of books,
The young ones just starting to learn,
Their life is beginning, so wondrous and new,
Their future so hard to discern.

Our mind is a mirror of images live
And so, fleeting the years travel by.
Before us soon stands our teenage youth,
With beauty one cannot deny.

The world is awake with the magic of life,
That glitters and beckons to thrill,
Of children at play, of laughter and love,
The promise of youth to fulfill.

A mother. a father, a title of honor
We struggle to always uphold,
Indelible memories each parent has
That become a part of our soul.

The Grandeur of life is a circle of love
With a child at the center of time
A symbol of hope for the whole human race
To guide us toward the divine.

Where are you this day?' Why have you gone?
Your loved ones, in dreams call out.
"We miss you so much that we hurt inside,"
Your family, in pain, seems to shout.

Our memories all come rushing back.
We hold you in our hearts.
You are with us now - and always.
The world cannot keep us apart.

You presence is so strongly felt,
We reach out with our arms,
And hold you close just one more time,
To keep you safe from harm.

We see you in our mind so clearly,
As if you are really there,
That we might reach with a loving hand
And tenderly brush your hair.

We hear your soft and gentle voice,
It speaks to all we have known.
We understand that you are here with us
And that you will never be alone.

Your laughter and your joy live on
To cherish through the years.
We are thankful for the time we had
As we struggle through the tears.

Your spirit lives within us
And it can never, ever cease.
Your memory, in love, a source
Of everlasting peace!

A Place Called Paradise

There is a place called Paradise, you can sometimes visualize
Some-where in a better world, where no one ever dies.
It is a place we meet as dreamers, where the sunlight never fades,
Some-where in a better world, where your heart is not afraid.

For the dread of saying good-bye, to those most dear to you,
Some-where in a better world, you should never have to do.
No, the loss of lives so sacred, especially in their youth,
Some-where in a better world, could never become the truth.

To feel the cruel and crushing pain, in losing their embrace,
Some-where in a better world, you would never have to face.
Yet we know if mankind's wish is true, there is a place of eternal peace,
Some-where in a better world, where happiness cannot cease.

Yes, there is a place called Paradise, with no illness, war or crime,
Some-where in a better world, where infinity measures time.
Here our loved ones live, in golden light, on a path many others have trod
Some-where in a better world, where our children walk with God.

A Simple Twist of Fate

There are times a person wonders when you start to contemplate,
How life can reach a turning point by a simple twist of fate.
Just the difference of a moment on the hands of heaven's clock
Can foretell the future pathway down the road of life we walk.

When it is said that fame and fortune favor the fearless and the brave,
Surely none can know their destiny from the cradle to the grave.
Still humanity seeks revelation, what luck will come to be,
But reality may unfold in ways they may not want to see.

There is such profound injustice in those never given a chance,
As they vanish from the halls of time - a victim of circumstance.
What message is mankind to learn, especially with those so young.
As we see misfortune strike them down and leave their lives unsung?

In the eternal eyes of innocence, with a newborn in our arms,
We can wonder what their future holds, as we pray, they are safe from harm.
But the ancient echo in answer to grief is the same as is heard still,
A prophetic mystery that defies the mind mere mortals call "God"s will."

The Dream

In dreams we find life's sacred loves,
Our deepest hopes and fears.
The magic of reverie transports time,
As we travel back in years.

I had a dream many nights ago,
so real it seemed quite odd.
But when I awoke, I felt as if
I had received a gift from God..

In my vision, I saw my only son
At a age of four or five.
He was just a little boy again,
But to me very much alive.

The fact that I had lost him
As a young man fully grown,
Played no part in this precious moment,
As we faced each other alone.

I picked him up into my arms
And looked into his eyes,
But as his father I knew his fate,
The tragedy he would not survive.

I lovingly gazed at my young boy
And could not hold back the tears,
A sobbing cry burst forth in pain,
As if within my soul for years.

He looked at me and spoke concerned,
"Daddy, why are you crying?"
And reached to brush the tears from my face
While I hid the sadness underlying.

I hugged him to my heart in love,
Saying everything would be all right,
His adoring eyes smiled up at me,
Then my dream began to fade from sight.

At times I think of this heartfelt vision
Where my son and I met in slumber,
And I am grateful for this memory of him
To heal a wound like no other.

Our dreams are like ships on the sea of life
As we sail toward the white light that shines,
Cherished thoughts in the midst of storm,
As we drift through perceptions of time.

THE COMPASSIONATE FRIENDS

Worldwide Candle Lighting

December 2006

Call to the Heavens

Let us gather on this eve of remembrance
To honor our children tonight,
The loved ones now taken from us,
As we join by the pale moonlight.

Let the golden flame of a candle
Light the way for our children above
To see their families below them
That we have come with our hearts filled with love.

May our Children find comfort this evening
As we stand in the cold night air
That their family is here to hold them
In their hearts forever with care.

Let our children know that we see them
In our mind as they smile from above,
That God's grace resides there with them
In the form of a snowy white dove.

May the children feel that we hear them
With their tender voices true,
As they speak to our hearts at this moment
On this candlelight rendezvous.

We call to the heavens for our children
That the stars be their guide tonight
Toward-the world's radiant candles
And the sacred warmth of light.

Thought we have lost our beloved children
And shed ten million tears,
The flame of love lit tonight
Will last for a thousand years.

Yes, this night we honor our children
Under a cathedral of stars so bright
As we light a simple candle
On this peaceful winter night.

May the gentle souls of our children
Sail on silver heavenly wings
Across the universe of our hearts and minds,
To live forever in our dreams.

THE COMPASSIONATE FRIENDS
Worldwide Candle Lighting
December 2007

Tears of the Soul

Let us feel the silence of sacred night
As we search our hearts from within
And remember the innocent children
Whose lives were once theirs to begin.

For the innocent are always with us
As we light the candle of life,
May it burn with the brightness of stars
And fill the heavens with light.

Let us take this moment for our young ones
As we light the candle of life,
May it burn with the brightness of stars
And fill the heavens with light.

Let us take this moment for our young ones
As we hold a candle for love,
May they hear our prayers and thoughts tonight
And smile down from the heavens above.

For their beautiful memories are still with us,
As we walk through the shadows of life,
We can hear them whisper, "I love you."
Even though they have vanished from sight.

Though we know, like the candle of our life,
That someday it will burn nevermore,
We need the innocent with us
So, our hearts may be helped to restore.

Still we hear the call of our young ones
And they tell us, "please don't cry,"
As the candle turns to misty smoke,
It is never really, goodbye.

For the innocent are always with us
As their spirit seeks to make us whole
Through the journey of a life
To heal tender tears of the soul.

The Garden of Peace

The Garden of Peace is a quiet place
Where the boy on the hill now sleeps.
Our Memories of him give comfort still,
As we struggle in our moments of grief.

The Garden of Peace is a solemn place
Where the boy on the hill can be found.
His life is cherished by his family each day
That we stand on this sacred ground.

The Garden of Peace is a beautiful place
Where the boy on the hill now dwells,
Trees tower heavenly toward clouds above.
While flowers cast a magical spell.

The Garden of Peace is a place in time
Where the boy on the hill now abides.
The courage he revealed in life live on
Like the sun and the ocean tides.

The Garden of Peace is a place of love
Where the boy on the hill lives still.
The hope and promise of his life so fresh,
All his needs we still yearn to fulfill.

The Garden of Peace is a place of tears,
Where the boy on the hill does lie.
What God has given, He has taken away,
And no one can tell us why.

GARDEN OF PEACE

Carousel of Dreams ~ Fleischer

In Loving Memory

Erik Alan Fleischer

1980   ~   2005

Some of Erik's drawings

Erik at camp Red Cloud

"If love could part
the silver clouds,
And golden angels be
my guide,
I'd fly right up to
heaven's gate,
And bring you home
again by my side..."
- Dad

Carousel of Dreams ~ Fleischer

Erik's letter found in his pocket:

"Dear Mom & Dad,
I'm sorry you guys have to go through this, but I've spent about seven years now stuck in the most horrible situation I could possibly think of and I can't do this anymore. I spent the first three years doing anything and everything I could possibly do to work through this. I put everything I had everyday into somehow getting back on my feet. These last few years have been pretty much hopeless because I can't see any way through this. This isn't just some anxiety I've been dealing with since high school. I've been living in mental anguish. I have trouble walking straight and talking straight. I can't think of any area of my life that this hasn't affected. These last seven years have been one long black misery for me and the thought of going on much longer makes me sick to my stomach.   I love you guys very, very much, but I have to be set free from this. Everything inside me longs to be free. We can't go back – but I have to go. Please be strong through this. It is my hope that you guys get through this. You, have to. There is no other way…"

-Erik

Our Dearest Erik,

We miss you in our life so much. You are loved and in our hearts every day. May God bless you and keep you safe in his arms forever.

All our love,

Dad, Mom, Heidi, Holli and Barbie

"This is the way I
want to be
remembered
before all of this
ever happened.
This is who I
really am."

Will We Meet Again?

It is when I'm alone

You drift quietly into my mind
I see your handsome face
I miss you
I love you
I hear my body breathing
My heart is beating

My eyes see, but you are not
there anymore. It is the
realization
That I can never see you again
That is so hard to accept.
Oh, my son, my son- Are
you truly gone forever?
Or will we meet again someday
And laugh and cry in the sunlight,
In the dawn of a new morning.

Dad

Christmas - 2005

Erik Alan Fleischer

April 26, 1980 - June 28, 2005

Life with the Dogs

Our two dogs Bella and Abby had become inseparable. Looking like Mutt and Jeff. Abby being Erik's dog, a medium size dog and all black. Bella was big and white with spots all over with two black ears and crystal blue eyes. Bella being the instigator of trouble. Beside the incident with chewing the bottom of the fence and escaping to roam the neighborhood, dear Bella was in the house when we decided to go for a late-night swim. She jumped up on the sliding glass door to let us know she wanted to join us since she liked to swim too, her paw came down on the latch and locked the door. The garage door was locked as well as the side gate. Our keys were in the house and that was before cell phones. It was far too late to yell at the neighbor, so we had to wrap up in the towels and tried to sleep on the lounge chairs trying to keep warm. Our daughter finally came home around 10am, asking us "what we were doing out there?" What indeed!

Another Move

After the sale of our house, we found a cute house to rent with a pool and in a cul-de-sac near the paseos where we could walk the dogs. Bella loved the pool. She would jump in and swim around, then get out and sun herself. Abby on the other hand, never did like the water and would not go near the pool. Our daughter had broken up with her long-term boyfriend and moved back home. She decided to go back to school, swearing of men for a while. Life continued with me working for Lexus and Larry with the State of California.

The Campout Party

Our daughter was busy going to school and working when she was invited by her x-roommate to a campout party for her 40th birthday. It was being held at a campground along the beach and she decided to go. Lo and behold she met a guy who they seemed to have a lot in common since she had lost her brother to emotional problems and his brother had gone through a lot of the same things as her brother. Turns out he was 15 years older. He was the brother of the birthday girl's best friend. He usually did not go with his sister anyplace but decided to go this time. They hit it off and she brought him home to meet us. He seemed very, nice. It was soon to be Barbie's 30th birthday and she decided to have a costume party. She and Gary had fun decorating the house and the outside patio for the party. He seemed to enjoy costume parties as much as she did. They dressed up as Cleopatra and him as Marc Anthony. Made such a cute couple. All their guests came in very clever costumes. It was a nice turn out and everyone seemed to have a good time. Turns out he was well established in his field of being a physical therapist at a major hospital in the valley. That is what she needed, we felt. Someone older and already working in his field of interest.   The   two   became inseparable.   He   joined   us   a Christmas, helping to put the lights up

and decorate the tree. We had a chance to get to know him better during this time and thought he was good for her.

Grandbaby #8 and a Wedding

After the holidays, in January 2007, I came home from work and checked the answering machine for messages and there was one from a

Dr.'s office calling for Barbie, saying something about her pregnancy test results. About that time, she walks in and hears the end of the message, sheepishly saying "I was going to tell you guys but didn't know how." So, it turns out she was pregnant with our 8th grandchild due in June…exactly 9 months after their meeting at the campout last September. Imagine that! It was decided they would get married after the baby arrived. So, she moved in with him a few months before our little

Serena Lynn ~ grandbaby # 8

granddaughter arrived on June 30th. They named her Serena. Plans had changed and they pushed the wedding forward to the following September 27, 2008. She wanted a wedding on the beach in Santa Barbara which took a bit of planning. It turned out to be a beautiful day with the ceremony set up on the grass overlooking the ocean. Two pillars with beautiful white flower arrangement were on each side, with a separation for the location of the vows. The reception was in the building behind where the chairs where set up. There was an oval patio with two trees on either side. Both, son-in-law's helped put twinkle lights in the tees creating a magical place to dance the night away after the ceremony. Family drove up and her sisters where her bridesmaids and granddaughter Kira, Kimi and Gary's daughter from a previous relationship where the flower girls. They looked so cute with their baskets and matching dresses. The tables inside were adorned with flowers made by a coworker where I worked. She did such a beautiful job. The tablecloths were aqua matching the overall theme. The twins wore beautiful strapless aqua gowns as well. My high school friend Fran and her husband supplied the champagne. Across the street was a beautiful carousel that they took pictures on and around. So magical!

The pictures taken on the beach with the bride and groom were amazing. The photographer was also a coworker of mine. She did such a wonderful job with the photos. Barbie enlarged many of them and has them on her wall in her new home. They look wonderful. Life was looking good.

Now with 9 grandchildren, we include Gary's daughter as one of our grandchildren as she is now part of the family.

Granddaughters
Annika, Kimi & Kira

Holli ~ Barbie ~ Heidi

Barbie and Gary's beautiful wedding - 2008

Losing my Mother

Mom had moved from Arizona to Missouri to be near my sister eventually, selling her home there and putting a manufactured home on my sister's horse ranch. Since mom had had a stroke and not quite recovered it was better to be near my sister so she could help if needed. As usual mom fixed her home up beautifully and made it so we all could come visit and be comfortable. She made the one big room into a game room with lots and lots of bookshelves, a fireplace, and a pool table for entertainment. Oh, and an oversized chess set that she had hand painted. She had two large china cabinets in the dining room filled with her china, silver, and crystal items. And all along the top of both units where rows of hand painted steins. When Serena was still a baby, Gary, Barbie, and I made a trip out together to see Mom. This was her sixth great grandchild and they wanted to be sure she got to meet her. We celebrated mom's birthday while out there. Dad came out with my brother and my sister's son and family came out as well. It was a nice get together. Mom was not doing too well after that and had to have a nurse be with her during the day while my sister worked. I would call and talk to her often but eventually she lost her hearing and would not come to the phone. She had to get around in a wheelchair at this point since it was painful for her to walk. When my sister came home after work, she would relieve the nurse. It was difficult lifting mom in and out of the chair she said. My sister was still going to horse shows around this time and unfortunately during one of the shows her horse had spooked and she was bucked off breaking her pelvis in 7 places. It became impossible for her to lift mom at this point because of her injury. It was decided by her and dad that it was time to put her in a home. Trying to make the room as homey as possible with a lot of her personal items around her as they could. She hated it and did not want to be there.

Sheila visited her often but one night the nurse called her to come quickly. She got there in time to be there when she passed, calling me and my brother with the news. She was 83. I felt so bad since we had not been out since the last visit. I miss her today and always. She was a special woman and made our childhood one of wonderful memories, like a "Leave it to Beaver" type home life.

Mom and I

Retirement and Another Move!

At the end of 2009 we decided to retire and found a 55+ community out in east Bakersfield about an hour away from Valencia. The homes in Valencia had become too expensive to retire with a high mortgage. Homes out there were half the cost, and something we could afford. They had a beautiful clubhouse with a café, ballroom, library, game room with pool tables, gym a movie theater, computer room, beauty shop and a craft room. Outside was a big firepit with chairs around it and stairs down both sides of  the patio where a waterfall was and the gates to go out to the big beautiful Olympic size pool surrounded with palm trees and a jacuzzi beyond the pool, as well as a lovely BBQ patio. It felt like you were staying at a resort. They had many activities for the residents such as dances for Halloween, Christmas, and New Year's. As well as craft fairs, car shows, pool parties and much more. We were sold and especially with the price of the brand-new homes. One such house we looked at had been lowered $20,000 making it the same price as one of the smaller homes. It was because it had been finished and all the houses around it had sold and they wanted to complete a sale on this last one for that block. The back yard had been done as well as the inside. It was 2,800sq ft which was a little large for two people but we thought it would be good for having the families over, all nine grandchildren and their parents as well as my dad who flew in from back east. It had a formal living room at the end of the long hall with floor to ceiling windows looking out the back. I put drapes separating them in the middle pulling to each side of the windows with ties.

At Christmas time we put a white tree in the middle. We had two pale green sofas, one on each opposite wall and a white baby grand player piano in the opposite corner. This was my gift to us from mom who left me some money. It is still my pride and joy and I listen to it while working on my projects. It is so relaxing, a delight to listen to. We bought it in September when we bought the house and moved it in first but waited until after our respective retirement parties and after we took a trip to Hawaii for nine days, to move in. It was such a wonderful trip. A second honeymoon of sorts.

We moved into our lovely new home in January 2010. We had views of the mountains and were 15 minutes east of Bakersfield and 8min from Ming Lake. It had a country feel as there was a farm on the other side of the back wall around the development. We would hear a cow or rooster every now and then.   In the winter we could see the snow on the mountains if it got cold enough. We were only 2 hours from Barbie and family and 4 ½ from the girls up in Sacramento. Sort of in the middle. This was good. And now to enjoy retirement.

Christmas at our new home 2010

A New Grandbaby

Our first year in our new home in Bakersfield was busy decorating and getting things put in their place. We were enjoying retirement, staying up late watching movies and sleeping in and not having to get up early to run off to a job was great. However, after six months of that we realized we did not have the extra money to go on our weekend trips like we use to. So, I went back to work. Was lucky to find a position with the Bakersfield Lexus. Larry decided with my friend Fran's help and encouragement, to purchase the new equipment to free-lance court reporting with an agency in town. Taking one or two jobs a week brought in good part time money. Now we could take a weekend here and there to go to Laguna Beach or to the wine country or drive to Solvang for the day. Christmas came and everyone came down to our new house. There was plenty of room for everyone including my dad who came out from Mississippi. The piano was wonderful playing all the holiday music in the background. My oldest grandson came with his girlfriend but has not been down since due to his job. He works every weekend, being a manger of his bike store and the busiest time of the year. We were so pleased he could join us this year.

2011 was busy with working our perspective jobs and attending Larry's kit collector shows two to three times a year in Anaheim. We would go to Knotts Berry Farm for their famous chicken dinner and to look through the unique shops, after the show, which I really enjoyed. And we went on our trips to Laguna Beach a couple times a year and went on a bus trip with our club house, to the wine country as well as attend the various parties they would have. The family came down for Christmas again this year each lighting a candle and saying what we were each grateful for, setting each candle down around an Angle figurine representing Erik. We have since added angles for all others we have lost. Barbie and Gary were expecting another baby by this time and on February 21, 2012 gave birth to another little girl. They named her Alana. This makes 10 grandchildren. I do think that will be the last. All are blessings to our life.

2012

2017

All our grandchildren except David - Christmas 2017

Diagnosed with Cancer

During 2012-2013 I was having a lot of pain from my back going down my right leg to the point I could hardly walk and was getting worse. However, during a routine mammogram done in early 2014 they discovered a lump. My world turned upside down. I received this news at my desk while helping a customer. I was expecting a call from the doctor and excused myself to take the call. In shock when the doctor told me, by phone mind you, I turned and collapsed into my coworker's arms sobbing. Someone else stepped in to help the customer. The General Manager heard me crying and came out to comfort me and sit me down. He was so kind and had someone drive me home following in my car. Larry was waiting outside for me and I ran to him and cried as he held me. Surgery was scheduled soon after on March 7th. The lump was so small all they had to do was a lumpectomy and radiation. Then I had to take a small pill for 5 years or more. Turns out 10 years now. All following exams turned out clear, thank goodness.

After surgery for cancer with my daughters

Back Surgery

After the surgery on my left breast, leaving a small indention, I was declared cancer free! Yah! However, as the year went on the back pain got worse. Finally cleared for surgery after jumping through all the hoops required by the insurance company, surgery was scheduled for October. Turns out it was a pinched nerve where the lower vertebrae had collapsed and was causing the pinching of the nerve. They needed to go in and open it up putting in a spacer bolting it in place. The surgery was a success! I realized then that the 2,800sq ft home was too much to maintain so we put it up for sale. We found a house around the corner that had just been completed except for the carpet and tile choices. It was only 2,000sq ft and much less work to maintain. So, we moved again, and hopefully for the last time!

First home in Bakersfield

A Smaller House

The new house was 3 bedrooms with a great room which was a living room/kitchen all in one. The master bedroom was large with an alcove window facing the back. A perfect place for a desk and my computer to work on all my projects. The bath had a large oval soaking tub which I really enjoyed. The middle room was to become Larry's man cave. He put in a nice desk with his large credenza to display all his airplanes, Nautilus, and other interesting items he collected. We also put a futon couch for guests with a coffee table. Pictures from the movie 20,000 leagues under the sea were displayed as well as the airplane pictures and other photos from movies he loved. A large movie poster framed of 2,000 Leagues Under the Sea was also displayed. A large beautifully framed photo of Walt Disney signed by Margaret Kerry, the lady who was Tinker Bell, also adorns the wall. Larry had always wanted to work for the Disney studios, however the war changed that for him. We decorated our new home in the sea-shore theme with light aqua carpet and lots of ship pictures and a large reproduction of a mermaid, one of our favorite photos. After moving 28 times in 37 years, we sincerely hoped this was the last move. I cannot help but think that all the moves we made did not help the kids. Especially Erik, the last child. Perhaps if we had not moved so much, things might have been different for him. We will never know. And all the crazy businesses we tried as well as all the homes we bought and sold, caused a very unstable atmosphere for our family. Yet the twins tell me they felt they had a wonderful home life and never wanted for anything. I guess we did something right.

I was fortunate that is how I remember my home life as well, thanks to my two wonderful parents. They did not divorce until much later in life. It was during this time that we found out our dear friend John was given less than a year to live due to a brain tumor that was inoperable. We were devastated to hear this news. Our dear friends who we went on so many wonderful trips with. They had become like family. The were there for the birth of our last two children and saw them grow up and the struggles we were having with our son who had been with us on many pool parties at their home during the summer. John will be so missed.

Life After Retirement

Going back a bit, in 2010 Larry's mom passed. She was 87. It was so hard on him. He was close to her all his life. However, they had moved out to Carson and we did not see them often. She was showing signs of dementia, not remembering where she lived. That was the year we moved to Bakersfield making us and hour further away.

 Retirement was good after we both were back to work and being able to escape on weekends to our favorite places.

A day at Laguna Beach

Francis Larry's beautiful mother

Heaven's Eternity

I hold your fragile hand in mine,
Eyes heavy with misty tears,
Your life is but a whisper now,
Time's dreadful tell of passing years.

Your body is still; your breathing shallow;
Your voice without a song.
The fear of final loss looms near
And I know I must be strong.

What can I say? What can I do
For the mother of my birth?
Was my lifelong love enough
To tell you of your worth?

Will you ever truly understand
All that you mean to me?
I yearn for an answer to my prayer,
Before my heart can set you free.

Memories crowd my mind with thoughts
Of our dearest days gone by;
Feelings in this twilight time
That I know will never die.

You open your eyes and there is love
Between a mother and her son.
For a moment two lives are joined in peace;
Together they are one.

I bow my head that at last you see
What your precious life has meant to me.
Your hand slips away from the love of mine;
I give you to heaven's eternity.

I love you, mom
Larry

The Twins Graduate & Dad turns 90

In 2015 Holli and Kie's twins graduated from Hight School. T.J. receiving an award for his participation on the baseball team, making the local papers, and Kimi for her cheerleading. We were so proud of these two. We went up for the graduation, participating in the celebration. The following year Heidi and Pats twins graduated, and we drove up for that event as well. The boys had done extremely well in Soccer over the years and Christian had hopes of a career in pro soccer. We were so proud of all four of their children and their accomplishments in soccer.

This July 31st Dad turned 90 and a family reunion was planned at my brother's lake house in Missouri.   My brother surprised dad by inviting his sisters six adult children who he had been close to over the years. Brought tears to his eyes when they came in the room one at a time giving him a big hug wishing him a Happy Birthday. I know it meant so much to him. Today he is 94 and doing well. Soon to be 95 but due to this virus and being house bound we are not sure about this year's celebration. We may have to have a virtual party or have it a few months later.

Kie and T.J.

T.J. receives an award for outstanding performance on the team.

Carousel of Dreams ~ Fleischer

Twins Christian & Brandon

Graduation Day

Twins Kimi & T.J. Graduates

Kimi our cheerleader

Dad's 90th Birthday

Another Loss

In 2016 on January 8th a tragic accident happened, taking the life of our dear Holli's husband at 49 years old. A long-time employee of UPS, he was crossing the yard at night to get his rig to start his shift when the vehicle that moves the rigs from place to place in the yard, came around the corner too fast and did not see Kie, running over him. He never had a chance. We were all devastated, especially Holli. He was the love of her life. They had a wonderful marriage of 23 years and were so happy. He was a wonderful father to David and the twins. He was involved in all their lives. T.J. and he were on the Japanese baseball team together for many years. It was so unbelievable. We drove up for the memorial still in shock that he could really be gone.

Memorial

The memorial was held in the Buddhist Temple where he and Holli were married. There was room for only 400 people. It turned out 1,200 came, standing in the hallways and outside in front. It was a cold drizzly day but all who could not get inside stayed outside to honor their friend and colleague of many years. They even brought his rig and parked it on the side. A stark reminder of his lack of presence and our loss. He was loved by so many. He had played on the Japanese baseball team since he was 16. The whole team came wearing their jerseys in his honor. Kies's mom and stepdad were on their way back from Arizona when they got the news. Kie was his mother's only child. His mother went into shock and had a stroke and was taken to the hospital upon arrival. They knew she would never forgive them if she was not at the memorial, so they had to check her out and bring her in a wheelchair for the service and take her right back and check her back in. She recuperated eventually after many months and seems to be doing better today. Holli spends a lot of time with her, helping with her speech therapy, taking her places, lunch, movies, nail salon etc. Such a loss, losing your only child. Our loss was devastating with Erik, so we understood the pain so well.

Hubby Gets Sick

One day in November 2015, we took a drive to Manhattan Beach for the day. We looked in some of the shops and then decided to walk down the hill to the beach to watch the sunset. Afterwards we left and proceeded to walk back up the steep hill when Larry seemed to have difficulty climbing back up and was struggling to breath. By this time, he had been dealing with a cough for years, but doctors all treated it like it was allergies. He took cough syrup to stop the cough every morning. I did not realize how serious an ongoing cough was. He set the appointment in January 2016 and after several tests and a C.T. scan of his lungs, we were told he had a rare lung disease. They did not know the cause and no known cure! His lung was closing up, and he only had 40% lung capacity. After coming home from Kie's memorial we had our annual in-home visit by a doctor from the insurance company and he could hear how bad Larry's lung was and told him to get a 2nd opinion. The doctor we went to just gave him inhalers which did no good. Larry never smoked, very seldom drank, seldom ate sweets (not like me) and always ate fish when we went out to dinner. He also maintained his weight his whole life. We made an appointment with a doctor in Valencia. And the minute he came in the room he said "I know what you have, I'm sending you down to UCLA for a possible lung transplant. The only thing that would fix this. By this time, he was on oxygen and carrying an over the shoulder rechargeable unit.   After many trips back and forth to UCLA and more tests done, they informed us that they could not help him because he had 4 blocked arteries. They could not put stints in the heart because the lung was to weak and the heart was not strong enough to withstand a lung transplant. He was told to put his affairs in order and that he had six months to a year. He was given a death sentence. My heart sank that day. I was going to lose my love, my soulmate at 71 and we would not grow old together I sat there in disbelief as my eyes welled up with tears. By this time, it was June.

We called the girls to give them the devasting news. I gave notice at my job and decided I needed to stay home with Larry and spend as much time as possible with him. Barbie our youngest refused to believe nothing could be done and did some research on the internet for something for her Dad.

Manhattan Beach 2015

Stem Cell Treatment

Turns out there was a procedure whereby they draw blood and wash it in a lab taking the stem cells out and putting them back in to you. This will rebuild the diseased lung with new stem cells, repairing the lung. The only place they did this was in Arizona and the insurance did not cover it. The cost was $7,500 of which we did not have. Meanwhile Larry was having difficulty walking anywhere and including out to the car. So, we got him a scooter of which I became quite proficient at taking apart and putting it back together when we would go places. He was able to plug his portable unit in the cigarette lighter in the car to charge it. At this point we started a GOFUNDME to raise the money and raised $8,000 from friends, family, and strangers. Bless them all. In October, packing up, we made the 9hour drive to Arizona and the Lung Institute located there. The hotel and food were included. The treatments were done over a three-day period. Our granddaughter Kimi was going to college there and came over to see us while we were there. She loved her papa and was so sweet to drive over. We really enjoyed her visit. Our hopes were high that this would repair his lungs in time.

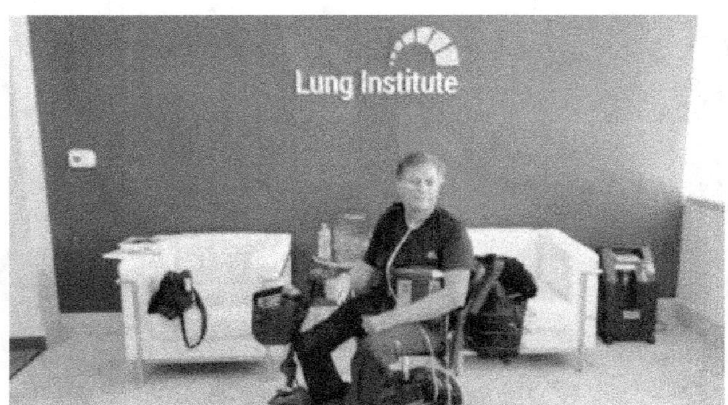

The Lung Institute ~ Arizona

Kimi comes to see Papa

Christmas 2016

Christmas this year, could be our last with Larry, so everyone came down to all be together. Photos taken with the youngest grandchild on his lap while on the scooter and a panoramic photo of everyone all together will be forever cherished. Larry's birthday was Christmas day 1945 and he was turning 71. Since we have several birthdays in December, Twins Heidi & Holli on the 21st, granddaughter Annika on the 17th and David our oldest grandson on the 9th. We put all their names on the cake and celebrated on Friday evening. Having our Christmas celebration, the next day, separating the two events. Larry was always cheated he said. Never had a party because all his friends were with their own families. He usually was handed and extra Christmas present saying it was his birthday present. No separate celebration. Our son-in-law, Gary would prepare a special dinner of fish on the 25th since we always came to their house for Christmas eve and Christmas day. Our family gathering was usually the weekend before.

New Year's came and we stayed in and watched the Dick Clark New Year's show, kissing at midnight and having a glass of champagne. As the weeks turned into a month, it was our 47th Anniversary on February 7, 2017. He insisted we go out, so I found B.J.'s had booths that had outlets so he could plug his oxygen system in while we ate. He was so sweet, he really tried to enjoy it and as he always did, would reach for my hands saying how much he loved me. I loved this guy so much and it was breaking my heart to see him looking so pale and not well. The waitress took our picture and you could see in the photo that he looked like he did not feel well. Makes me sad, it has me crying just remembering that day.

This was the last time he saw his sister, in the bottom right photo, taken on one of our trips to UCLA as well

Our 47th Anniversary dinner

Alana with Papa

Happy Birthday Heidi, Holli and Larry

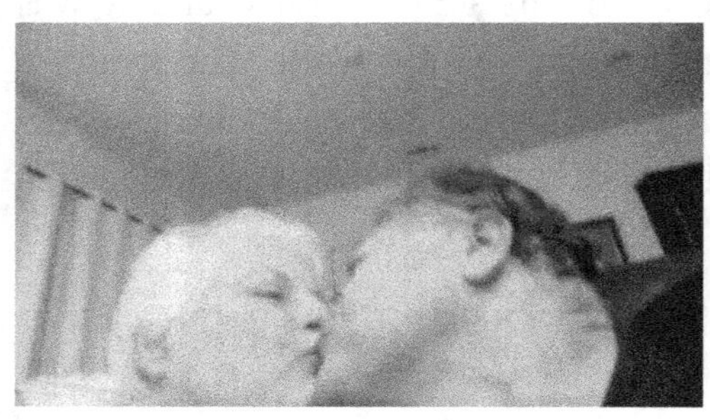

Happy New Years sweetie

Larry and sister Joan

Another Trip to Arizona

We decided to make another trip to Arizona for a 2nd stem cell treatment to give him that extra a boost. After raising more money from another GOFUNDME we raised the $6,500 needed for the next treatment. We were going this time at the end of February. It seemed by now, Larry could not drive because he had to keep his oxygen regulated and it required his full attention. I then became the driver. I was so nervous having to drive through the Los Angeles traffic.   As we started out, we had not gotten far when the cigarette lighter failed and was not charging. We turned around and went to our mechanic. He said he could not get the part until Monday. We could not wait. We had to be in Arizona by tomorrow, Sunday. He improvised and hooked it up another way. On the road again, and driving several hours, we decided to stay at a hotel overnight and cross the border in the morning. We checked in late Sunday, arriving early morning for the first treatment. The treatments went well over a two-day period this time. Kimi came to visit again. We always enjoy seeing her. We left Wednesday morning but shortly before the border into California, the cigarette lighter failed again. I pulled off at the nearest hotel and got Larry out and into the lobby and got his machine plugged in.   I then found a Lexus dealership and drove to them to see if they would order the part and repair the car. They were so nice and said they could and gave me a loaner. Driving back to the hotel we had to check in for the night.

The next morning after making sure Larry was ok, I drove back to the dealership only to find the wrong part was delivered. What else could go wrong? Fortunately, the manager told me that there was another outlet in the back near the floor of the center divider. Thank goodness, we were saved. Driving back to the hotel, I picked up Larry and we were on our way again. However, after getting a bite to eat and some gas it was getting to be late. By the time we reached the California boarder it was getting dark. I did not like driving at night. By the time we reached the 210 it was very dark. I was so nervous, gripping the steering wheel so tight and my shoulders being tense because of the oncoming traffic and the bright on coming lights. It was a long drive until we finally got to Valencia. I was exhausted from the tension of the drive. We made it home at 10pm.

Hospital Stay

It was now the beginning of March and Larry was so drained from the last Arizona trip, he had become bedridden, and said it was taking too much oxygen and effort to ride the scooter to the bathroom and asked me to order a port-a-potty for the side of the bed. He was needing more and more oxygen as well. I prepared his meals and brought them to him. He was sleeping a lot. I think because of the pills that the doctor gave him were the cause. For a person who barley took aspirin, these large capsules of which he had to take 9 a day was difficult for him. They were supposed to slow the disease down. One day he was really struggling with his air and I pushed the emergency button and the ambulance took him to the hospital. They did several tests on him and the doctor said he had had a mild heart attack. I was with him there for a week. I insisted he be brought home by ambulance because I felt nervous taking him home in the car. A nurse came to the home twice a week and a physical therapist came to help keep his upper body in physical shape. Still struggling with not getting enough oxygen, I called the company who supplied the oxygen to get more and they said a doctor had to order it. I called the doctor then and the nurse said Larry had to come in and be seen. I was so upset with her. I said "He can't come in he just got out of the hospital and is to weak. He needs more oxygen!" The doctor called it in, and the oxygen company came that afternoon. He now had two big units connected by one cannula giving him double the oxygen. All three girls came down that following weekend to see their dad and to spend time with him. He was grateful. He was getting so thin by this time. Apparently when you are sick your food does not metabolize as well.

Passing

On March 28th I had turned a movie on for us to watch. Suddenly he needed more oxygen, so I got up to help him and turned the oxygen meters up as high as I could. He asked me to bring the cannula from the big tank from across the room and turn it on as well. It seemed he was struggling to get the masks on his face, so I pushed the emergency button. He asked me to hold his head up, he could not do it himself. He then said, "I cannot do this anymore." He was perspiring profusely, and I saw his hand twitch and then he stopped breathing. The Life Alert people were still on the line and instructed me to make sure he was lying flat and to start to push on his chest until help came. The paramedics arrived shortly after and took over. My neighbor came over to be with me. She was my emergency contact since she lived next door and my children were all too far away. I knew even before the paramedic came out kneeling before me, saying they could not revive him, that he was gone. I was in shock, not wanting to believe it. They brought him out on the stretcher for me to say goodbye. I kissed him on the cheek, giving him a hug and whispering in his ear. "I will always love you." Then they took him away. My neighbor invited me to stay at her house overnight, which I was grateful for. I did not want to be alone that first night. My soul mate was gone. This is so hard reliving another overwhelming loss. I could not believe it. He was way too young.

How would I go on without him?

First Year

My neighbor made calls to my girls, letting them know of their dads passing. They were all devastated, and I was so grateful they came down the weekend before to see him. We had high hopes for his recovery. When we were in the emergency room at the hospital a couple of weeks before, an emergency room doctor heard us talking about the stem cell treatment Larry had gone through and came over to talk to us about it. He said he had been working in the field of stem cell treatment and felt it was the way of the future. Unfortunately, it takes time for the stem cells to rebuild, that you would need a year at least and 2 to 3 treatments. Larry just did not have time on his side. But at least we tried. They say his condition could have been hereditary. I really thought we would grow old together. It was not meant to be, I guess. I called my girlfriend Fran, from high school, telling her what happened. She drove out from Torrance, to be with me during these first few days. We had a lovely memorial at our Clubhouse ballroom. Family and friends came from all over. My brother came out and gave me $5,000 to help with the expenses. I will forever be grateful for not only his presence and representing the family but for his financial help during this difficult time. My granddaughter Kira made a lovely video of Larry and I from when we met and through the years done with all our favorite songs. Brought tears to everyone's eyes. I was in a daze that day. Could not seem to talk to anyone. Erik's friend Josh was there and helped a lot. My friend Fran sang Larry's song "Somewhere over the Rainbow." She and her husband provided the food as well. Our old neighbor insisted on providing the wine and served it as well. The speaker was one of the club members and he kept things flowing. I spoke thanking everyone for coming and to those who helped. My neighbor Patti sat at the table at the entrance greeting everyone and asking them to sign the guest book. Other members were so gracious to help decorate the room. It turned out so beautiful with flowers on the tables and our photos laying loose around them and the flowers around the urn as well as a heart arrangement with a sash across the heart with "In our hearts forever." My brother spoke at the end, where I introduced him to those who did not know him, thanking him for all his help and for being here for me.

We had a graveside service in Valencia a couple months later and a few friends and family came. After wards having a lunch at Larry's favorite Chinese restaurant. Everyone went home to their lives and I was alone. I muddled through the days without Larry, missing him so much. It was soon to be my 70th birthday in November and I decided to take my girls to Hawaii to celebrate and have some alone time together, something we have not had much of. I am so grateful for their husbands in holding down the fort during the week we were all away. Landing in Hawaii November 4th we had to rent me a scooter since my back was again giving me a lot of pain when walking. We ate at the Cheesecake factory and I got a piece of cheesecake for my birthday. My favorite! We then flew to Mau to Hollis timeshare for a week. They had a cake and flowers and a beautiful card waiting on the table and some chocolate strawberries. We had a wonderful time.

We took a dinner cruise, saw a Luau, drove the 17mile drive and enjoyed the beach and pool. We took lots of photos returning home rested and happy we made the trip.

In December everyone came to my house for the holiday.
It was sad that Larry was not with us. Our first Christmas without him.

We continued our tradition of sitting in a circle and lighting a candle and saying what we were each grateful for. It came around too little Alana who was 5 at the time. And she said, "I am grateful to have been able to play with papa." As she started to cry. We all cried then. She really missed her papa. We would set the candle on the table around an angel representing Larry. We added one for Kie and Pat's dad who passed shortly after Kie and an angel for Erik. We have kept the tradition every Christmas we get to together.

Carousel of Dreams ~ Fleischer

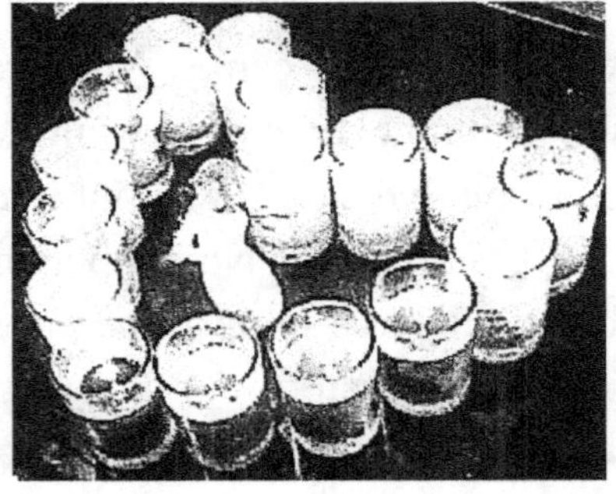

The Memorial for Larry

Hawaii ~ 2017

Second and Third Year

This next year I was busy with a few more trips. Trying to stay busy and to not think of being without my love. In July, the girls and I went to Mississippi for my Dad's 94th Birthday. We again went to my brother's new lake house. We went jet skiing and swimming in the oh so warm lake and just had a wonderful celebration with Dad who is doing well for his age.

I had mentioned to my girlfriend Fran that what I missed was our weekend trips we used to take all the time. I would not go alone. That is no fun. My dear friend said she would take me on a trip to Laguna Beach, which was one of our favorite places to go to. We stayed at a beautiful place on the ocean with a wonderful ocean view. The water came up right under our balcony. We had a lovely dinner in the restaurant at the hotel and the next day walked down to the town and looked around at the shops, having lunch at the village café over-looking the water. Larry and I had been there so many times. It was a beautiful day. I did have to stop frequently due to my back, however. It was a wonderful weekend and I will always be grateful to Fran for that kind gesture and telling me it was her treat. I will always be grateful for her friendship all these years and being there for me no matter the need. It has been a friendship spanning over 56 years. That is a long-devoted friendship I will always cherish. Then my other friend from Santa Barbara who is also a widow since John passed a few years ago, asked if I wanted to take a train to San Diego for a week. It sounded great to me. We stayed at a hotel across from the Old Town which we walked around before taking the trolly down to the harbor. We took a lunch cruse out to see all the many seals. Returning we got on the trolly again driving around San Diego. It helped I did not have to walk much. We stopped a few places and then would get back on the trolly and go to the next stop. We ended up getting off in Little Italy and having dinner at an Italian restaurant. Had the best spaghetti I have ever tasted. One day we went to their mall and had lunch at The Cheesecake Factory, the best Chinese chicken salad ever. In August, T.J. my grandson got married and he became a stepfather to his new wife's 3yr old son. It was a lovely wedding up in Sacramento.

On December 14th his twin sister, Kimi graduated from college in Arizona. The girls and I flew there for the beautiful ceremony. I was thrilled I could be there for her. I am so proud of her accomplishments.

The following year she applied with the airlines and is now a flight attendant and loving every minute of her job. Although furloughed for a month due to the virus for now.

Also, during this year our little Serena and Alana were in a darling dance recital both doing a wonderful job. There striped black and white outfits were so cute.

Christmas came around so fast and was again at my house. Even though the house was smaller, we managed to make room for everyone. T.J. and his wife came, and Christian brought his girlfriend. In all there were 17 of us. It was so nice having everyone home for the 2nd Christmas without Larry. Again, we honored all those who were not with us and lit a candle saying what we were grateful for this year. In 2019 I made trips to Simi Valley for birthdays of the two youngest grandchildren and made a couple trips up to Sacramento. Taking the train one time and drove the other. Granddaughter Kira graduated this year. She was so adorable taking photos with her cap and gown holding her little pug, Buttercup.
It was also Annika's graduation, Gary's daughter, and I drove down with Barbie and family to Long Beach for that ceremony. Her mother treated us to a lovely dinner afterwards.

After suffering with my back for a few years, I finally got a surgery date in November. It turns out the two vertebras above the one I already had operated on had collapsed and was pinching nerves. The surgery was successful, and I had no more pain, being able to walk again. I had a good surgeon and would recommend him to everyone with this kind of problem.

After coming home from the hospital, Bella was not doing well, not eating and looking very thin. She was almost 16 and slept all the time. It was time, sadly, we had to let her go. We had a little memorial on November 26, before taking her down to the vet to lay her to rest. We miss her so much.

Christmas this year was going to be at our daughter Barbies new house. The theme was a Masquerade Ball. This year it was after Christmas but before New Year's.

Her new home looked beautiful. She had gold and black decorations with a center piece with black feathers and a gold tall champagne glass. The game room was filled with black and gold balloons hanging from the ceiling. There was a taco island in the kitchen and lots and lots of champagne. Everyone dressed the part and wore black and gold or red and all wore masks. We danced the night away and all had a great time. It was a great ending to 2019. However, I really missed my dance partner.

Photos from 2018-2019

My beautiful daughters

2019 Masquerade Ball at Barbie's

Barbie & Holli jet skiing at
grandpas Birthday in Missouri

2018-2019 photos continues...

Serena & Alana's performance

Dad's 94th Birthdy

Annika Graduates

Kimi Graduates

Kira Graduates

My trip to Laguna Beach with friend Fran

Christmas 2018

My trip to San Diego with Suzie

Grandson T.J. gets married

Christmas 2019

Memorial for Bella

In Conclusion

Returning home on January 2nd of this year, it hit me, this lonely feeling in the pit of my stomach. So I decided to write this book about my life and all that we had been through with losing our son and the many others we lost along the way, with the greatest loss being the love of my life before our life was even over. One of the things Larry said to me before he passed was "I guess my book will never get published." I decided to add our story to his poems to publish it as our complete story in hopes it will help others who may have had similar events that happened to them and how we dealt with this difficult and tragic event of losing a child. Now that Amazon has created a way for people to publish online for little cost by self-publishing, I thought I should at least try to fulfill Larry's dream.

2020 is going to be accomplishing projects I have put off for some time and fill my days more constructively. I've recently printed photos out to put in a scrapbook like I used to do many years ago before I started making books on-line with my photos of the grand kids birthdays and other special events, giving them as gifts. There is something rewarding in making a scrapbook using creative stickers and colored paper. I have completed 2017 and 2018 and will end up with 2019's wonderful trips and get-togethers with family and friends. This year may not be as interesting since we are all quarantined and cannot travel to see family, therefore no pictures. However, I did find out my grandson who married in 2018 is expecting a baby girl. This will be my first great-grandchild. Hopefully by the time she is born in October I will be able to see her.

It is a scary time in our life with this deadly coronavirus spreading from city to city, country to country. A worldwide epidemic. Our generation has never experienced anything like this where all the stores are shut down except grocery stores, pharmacies, and gas stations. The highways empty except a few. And it looks like it is going to go on until June or longer. The schools are closed, and the children are taking virtual classes online and the doctors appts. are on skype. I fear it is going to be a slow recovery when all is said and done.

I received a call last Sunday, what would have been my sons 40th birthday, from a friend of my husbands who was a counselor for kids that were troubled and were on medication for similar conditions as Erik had and he told me not to feel guilty for not doing enough to help Erik because Erik was born with the gene and there was nothing I could do to change it.   In boys it usually shows up around 17 of which is when it did for Erik. What happened with him and his struggles would have not changed.

I felt a little better knowing this fact and not realizing it. Somewhere along the line of Erik's treatment one doctor said he was schizoid personality i.e., emotionally cold, detached, apathetic. I know he always seemed uptight and cold. I think because he was always focusing on what was going on in his mind. He could only relate to one person at a time and not even that later on. I don't think he was apathetic, fearful that he we would end up like a vegetable in a coma, yes. I knew him best but yet I didn't understand him. I was with him the most, taking him to his appointments, yet I didn't know him at all. I could not seem to reach him. Maybe I was to busy with all that went on in our life with moving, side businesses, raising the others that I did not really see him. I know he did not blame us but seemed grateful for everything we tried to do realizing that there was no hope for a normal life.

His notes I found explains a lot. Heart breaking details of what he was going through every day of his life. We felt so helpless that we could never fix it for him. Make life better for him. He tried so hard those first 3 years when he was first diagnosed. Determined to not take medication and fix it on his own. But it was not to be. His condition just got worse which is evident by the two follow up suicide letters written in 2001 and 2002 and ultimately the last one in 2005.

But the questions are still, why him? Why did my son have to come down with this devastating disease? A question that will never be answered.

Hopefully, the fact that you are reading this now, means I have succeeded in bringing my love's dream come true. I hope you found the poems and our story inspiring and in some small way a help in your own struggles with a child suffering from this condition.

My dearest Larry

The moment that you left me

My heart was split in two

One was filled with

Memories The other
died with you.

I often lay awake at night

When the world is fast asleep

And take a walk down memory lane

With tears upon my cheeks.

Remembering you is easy

I do it every day
But missing you is a heartache That
never goes away.

I hold you tightly within my heart
And these you will remain

You see, life has gone on without you
But will never be the same.

With all my love,
Rita
(Author unknown)
In loving memory of the author:
Larry L Fleischer
December 1945 - March 2017

Father and Son at peace together

Erik's Notes:

The following are notes written by Erik during the 7 years that he suffered with the disease Schizophrenia and that I had never seen before. They were heart breaking to read especially with this being Mother's Day weekend. They show just how much pain he was in. I do not think any of us realized just how much pain he really was in with this mental illness and the struggles he went through trying to find a solution to fix it. There is correspondence with his father as he turned to writing his feelings down instead of talking. He wrote two other suicide notes, the one in 2001 was when he stole the gun and could not go through with it. The second in 2002 with the last one written in 2005 when he succeeded in taking his life.

11-21-01

Dear Mom + Dad.

I just wanted to say thank you for buying me the tapes and everything but just because they're not helping me doesn't mean that I just need to keep drumming them into my head. It just means they're not applying to my situation. And I think you guys sense the hopelessness of my situation but are afraid to admit it. And I don't blame you. No parent wants they're kid in this situation but its a reality that I've had to live with for three years now. This condition didn't just settle in 6 months ago, I've been fighting for my life for 3 years proactively + done a lot (and I mean A LOT) to try and solve this problem.

To be honest, it kind of saddens me that you guys didn't want to keep close attention to how I was overcoming my problems back when twistjon was helping me these 2½ years. I would constantly drop hints but it seemed like you just expected twistjon to solve it. and by doing so you completely missed all the things I was doing to try and conquer this. Getting jobs at resteraunts, going out for basketball, the swim team, Colorado, everything, and it seemed like you acted like everything was fine. Well it was not fine and I will be damned after I'm gone that after all that hell I went through, alone, was wasted for nothing. And yes I'm informed, I'm very informed and you could find that out simply by talking to me. I know what a good therapist is because I would make a good therapist.

I grasp what a good adolescence is and how to break free of that into adulthood. And my adolescence has

has been off for years, far beyond when I was 17, but nobody ever knew it. Well the past is in the past and theres no changing that but I can't live like this anymore, Its a lonely sad, sickening, existance and I'm not going to wait around until you guys realize it. why? because that means I'm a ticking time bomb and if you realize that or my probation officer realizes that then that means I suffer the consequences. Wal I've suffered enough and I can't take this anymore. I have to go. Good bye.

Jan 6, 2002

1

Dear Mom and Dad,

Even as I speak I grow increasingly unstable. I'm so afraid of what I've become, I think you guys sense the hopelessness of my situation but are afraid to admit it. And I don't blame you. No parent ~~what~~ wants there kid in this situation but its a reality I've had to live with for three years no,,and a half years now. This situation didn't tick in just six months ago, I've been battling for my life for over ~~three~~ years now and have done an incredible amount to try to solve it.

These years with Kristjon were a frantic ~~xxxxxxx~~ pursuit for my life. It didn't seem like any family was really in touch with it at the time so I ^I know it^ went unoticed. ~~xxx~~ Getting jobs at restcraunts, going out ~~for~~ swim ~~team~~ backetball team, colorado, everything. Any attempts now will only be an extension of what I've already tried and I'll be damned if people say I just didn't want

2

to try. I wish their was some simple solution like medication or something but but the truth is my reality seems to be sorely distorted and it scares the shit out of me everyday. And since Josh had left things have gotten steadily worse but the situations a total catch twenty two. I can't live with my friends and can't live without them. Its a sad, lonely, sickening, existance and it has a very good chance of getting a lot worse. In fact it already has.

I wish things weren't the way they are. I'm sorry for making such a mess out of things. I should have just ended it when I was seventeen. I wish seventeen never even happened but the things that happened have already happened and theirs no turning that back now. You guys did the best you knew how. I'm not perfect and your not perfect. We all only knew what we knew at the time. When I was seventeen and I started to go crazy I only handled it the only way I knew how and you guys handled it the only way you knew how. Now that bridge has already been crossed and theirs no turning back.

But that still doesn't change things for me. Don't think their was anything you could have done to stop me. Its much too late for anyone to help me at this point and my only concern is that I end this thing before its too late. I can't keep living like this and I cant live in a mental institution, I'm sorry

Please, please, please just honor my life by pulling together as a family and really seeking to get the help you need. You must do this because theirs other people that need you. And I would like to ask that you would celebrate my death, Like you would celebrate a person with cancer. A person thats consumed in pain and is now resting in peace. mine just happens to be one of mental illness and is by far, much worse. At least with cancer your psychological is still in tact. Believe me, I know what I'm talking about! It all just seems a tragic twist of bad luck,

I will love you always. I know I had a hard time showing it but its true,

E,k

P.s. - And don't let any religous fanatics tell you anything because before God, I have done everything I could.

P.SS.- Please don't be sad. I know if you could visually see how bad things are you would have relief as I have relief. If only you guys knew! If only you guys knew......
I cant even sleep any more without waking in a panic. let alone living. Its so selfish for people to guilt me into staying.
"time is the ultimate healer." They just don't understand.

I've always maintained that this situation is getting worse always. Thats what buying the car was all about. Now that things are where they are now You guys think its the medication but I've always said it's getting worse always its just now ~~starting to look fr~~ How can even Basta say what I've taken everything He gave things were always the same or worse It just so happens the ability was what I was taking at this point. But Back when driving got harder you would Say It was because I stop taking what I was taking back then. But I've continued taking the same things all along.

whether I like it or
not it is the way
is (the last 7 years
shows that)

— The reason why was
I knew I was stranger
then because it wasn't
~~still~~ as bad back then
lie: I could still go. places
and do things
~~I feel~~ the pressures of
(at first made me think
that) but Josh's visits ~~at~~
~~really~~ visits at
hanging out with
helped things

technique &

skills in managing 5

family support groups

accurate information

problem solving skills

communication

judgmental & critical
will make them worse

sense of isolation

If you don't take meds,
you will end up pushing yourself
into a psychotic event will

I Love you guys so Much.
I wish you guys didn't have
to go thru all this but
as long as I live you guys
would have too.

I love you guys
very much. and I'm
begging that you guys
be strong thru this. There
is nothing we can do
to go back. whats
happened has happened
I must go. I really tried.
I love you guys.
If you guys loved me you
would want this for me, to
end the suffering.

I just wanted to include this photo because
It just means so much to me. To be honest, I was
miserable that whole summer but thats just because these
last three years have been misery. But even in the midst of
that I managed to go to this absolutely beautiful place, and for
the first time, experiance real change. change of scene, change of
activities, and the responsibily of living on my own. And by
forcing myself to live and ~~get to know all these~~ get to know all these
knew people, that were my age, and a blast to hang out with,
I managed to bring back memories that I cherished. A very fun
and youthful spirit ran through it all and it made me joalous
for life. It was one of the few times I can remember
being around that giddiness that comes with being a teenager.
Not as a spectater but accepted. ~~and even though~~ and even though mentally things didn't change, it
~~taught~~ taught me a lot about life. I don't know why I'm
saying all this but I guess I just feel like expressing
the things that meant the most to me and I'm sure your
all wondering, "why didn't he just move back!" but thats not the
answer. I truly belive my mind has become sick
and ~~theres~~ nothing that can change that. Like I wrote
in the letter, I'm a ticking time bomb waiting to explode!

In 98' the breakdown
distorted my thoughts
in a time mine are

Fear is
very treatable
growing increasing
as true
I worse
goes on
everyday I right
everyday because I
a lot wanted to get turned
around but I couldn't

If your wrong I could
        spend the rest of
I'd my life ~~that~~

I pushed myself through
everything school, work
church

- dad ~~I told~~ you
  you said that you guys
  aren't going to do anything
  ("nothings going to happen ~~to~~
  were not going to do anything")
- You could read my
       last letter

The problem is that
~~dealing with later~~ doing
more stuff is going to bring
on more stress which I
don't know I can deal with.

~~I grow is~~
I'm not "just getting" myself
worked up ~~to~~
- I'm growing worse as time
goes on.

as time went on.
  - driving
  - going out etc.

~ its messing with something.
  its hard to talk about

theres something you need those
to stand trial   are
                             my
                             Symtoms!

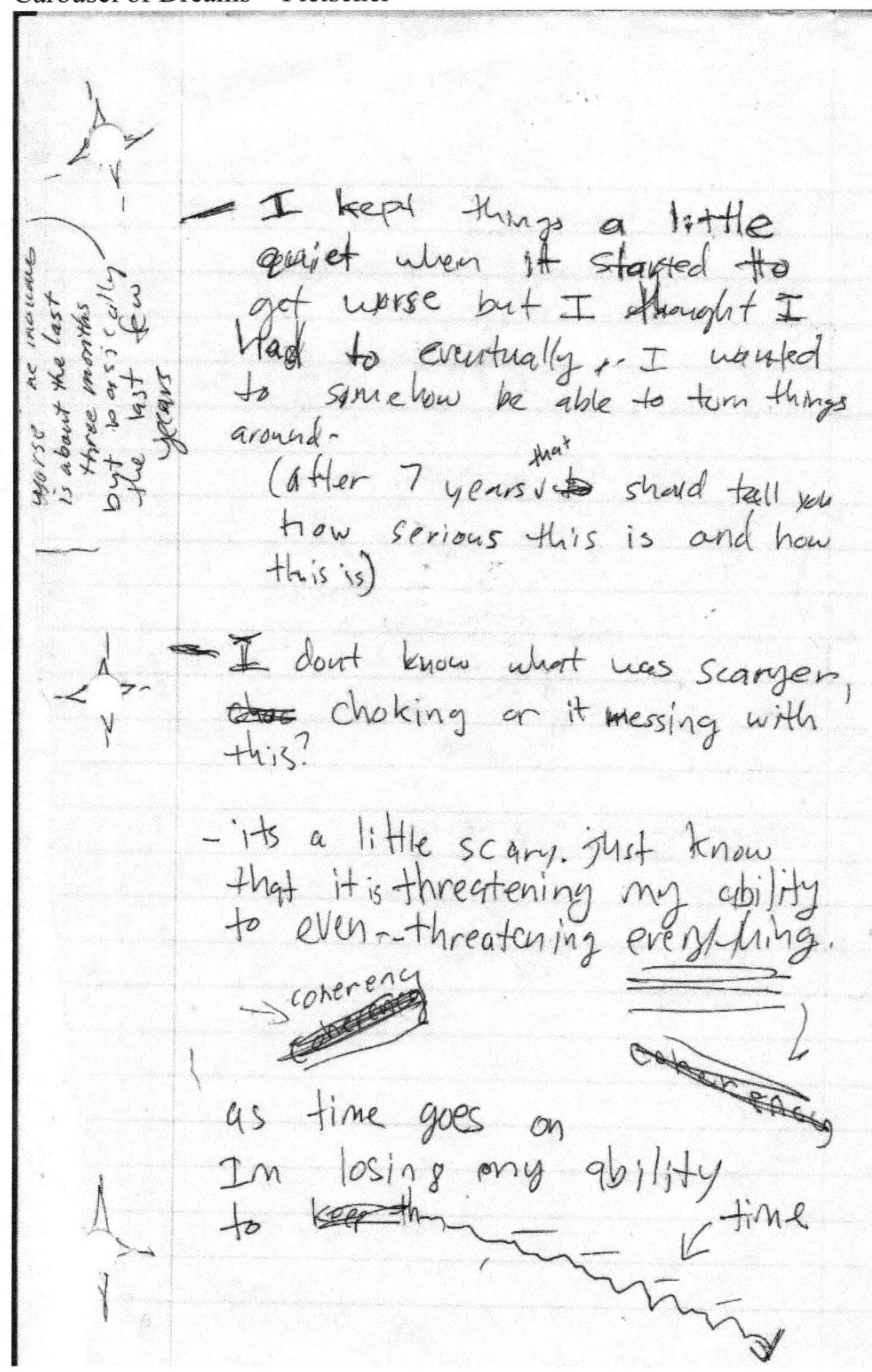
worse as indicate
is about the last
three months
but basically
the last few
years

- I kept things a little
quiet when it started to
get worse but I thought I
had to eventually. I wanted
to somehow be able to turn things
around.
(after 7 years that should tell you
how serious this is and how
this is)

- I dont know what was scaryer,
choking or it messing with
this?

- its a little scary. Just know
that it is threatening my ability
to even--threatening everything.

coherency

as time goes on
Im losing my ability
to   time

I remember 2004 because I bought the grind rail in christmas 2003 and after ~~then~~ a couple of months after driving became very very difficult.

I continued to fight that throughout the year because that was the last great pleasure I could really enjoy.

I ~~still can't believe~~ how ~~long I was driving~~

I didn't want to be drivin places because it made me feel like a little kid but I gradually had to accept it.

— this situation
been getting worse
since the beginning
but in the last
month it's got harder

— I've slowly lost abilities
to do things over
thing like driving
going etc. because
it's just gotten to
harder to deal with
the way it is

= In the past
I remember it
exactly when
started getting much
more difficult (early 2004)

11

- I think you guys
know my life more
then anyone.
You know where I go
and what I do pretty
much all the time
cant you guys basically
answer these.

- my days and nights
have been getting worse
all week but thats just
the way its been going
Im fighting because I
want to enjoy things but
I dont know

my life is made up of doing practicaly nothing thoughout my day. I have an all consuming problem that effects everything I do. You could put me in any situation and its diffcuilt thats because of my situation.

You would probably check
always or offer for all
the ones I didn't check
not because I struggled with
the situations but that I'm
struggeling with everything
as a result of my situation

= I always said "this
Situations serious" but I
think It wasn't as
evident att first.

— J

= I wish I could just relax
like before.

= Its not the way this
thing works. I wish I
could sometimes have a
drink or take something
but its not that way.
~~always~~ I wish to God it
was. That would be simple

ON DRIVING!

- Just ~~as~~ I'm struggeling to cope with ~~this thing~~

Coping with my situation over time got harder and harder on the road to where reacting to cars and stuff got very difficult.

- back then that was bad but as time went on other things like ~~[crossed out]~~ basic stuff got hard

- I think this was a situation ~~that everyone~~ kind of had ~~to deal~~ in ~~the beginning~~ but has ~~bee~~

- Mom, I ~~can~~ can't keep having

- My problems never got
easier over time they
always got more difficult

We say that everyday
but

- Dad I'm fighting
not for pete but
for myself I cant
bare this getting worse.

→ Are you guys scared
of what happens if
things continue.

- It wouldn't matter if
docters can understand
it if that's nothing
they can do. They
understand Aids but
cant do.

Dad, All these years of
going to Basta's and how
hard that was, honestly with
the way I am now I
don't even see that as
possible anymore Even
that got harder over
time. why could we
make that easier? my
problems obviously very
abnormal why couldn't we
make make seeing Basta
easier?? and I can
tell you, I'm ten times
worse now. Just the
fact I'm having to
write responses should
say something.

ERIK, there is always a choice, EVEN IF IT'S JUST A MENTAL CHOICE TO FACE YOUR GREATEST FEARS HEAD ON AND BE WILLING TO DO ANYTHING THAT WE, YOUR PARENTS, THINK WILL END THIS WAY OF EXISTING.

IF YOU THINK SOMETHING BAD WILL HAPPEN ANYWAY, ARE YOU WILLING TO MAKE A MENTAL CHOICE — TO CHOOSE THE POSSIBILITY, THROUGH OUR LOVE AND TRUST, TO GAIN A NEW LIFE?

I have to ~~fight~~ no matter what ~~it this~~ I'm no one else but myself. I've got no choice and if these last seven years have proven anything its that this is the way it is. If it wasn't I could just get up right now take myself out to dinner and stay out all night. but thats never been the case and You've seen it

— its the choice between ~~Stuff~~ you guys losing me or You guys losing me. I continue to only suffer

— I don't anyone to get in trouble

— wouldn't be great to just in I don't know Im just sick of dealing with things

— If I go to the hospital or whatever ~~it~~ it will only be bad I wish would just stay and talk about things. I know its exausting. I know but I think this is a very important time.

— I think that just right now is important just in terms of how ~~eat~~ ~~this~~ things are right now.

— I think we're all had a lot of time to put things off and even if we spent a lot of time tonight dealing with this I think it would be worth it.

- Can you get mom I think we need to talk more ~~to talk more~~
- I just wish things werent the way they are but this ~~is~~ is like the hand that we dealt
I feel like one option bad but the others worse.

~~options~~

2 options

1 Bad
1 worse

I wish I could comfort everyone right now ~~to I~~
~~listened to eve~~

I think this B exausting to deal with. I know but I thinks its important. ~~this~~

It seems
to me that
mine is more of
a distortion

struggling
with
control

in light of the Josh
situation what can I
do?

I think on paper
alot of ~~them~~ docters talk
about illnessesor a whatever
but I think everyones
is specific mines
like this

when the psychologist
say "illness" that
generic because they
can't explain each case
its all too ~~s~~ complicated or weird
but their catagorised
~~th~~ like this.

If you had to choose between bringing this situation to a conclusion (ending up the way you think you will)

OR

Choosing the possibility of returning to a normal life and recovering from this mental prison,

which would you choose?

Without a shadow of a doubt to be free but I have fought my guts out since 98' and ~~everything I know~~ and is ~~the~~ fought my guts out ~~a~~ to keep what I've had

No, But I think it comes in many forms but its all basically ~~disguised~~ the same labels the put on it.

- I dont feel like I have to ~~Just~~ stab in just any direction. The situation is more desperate now.

- I don't feel like ~~op~~ my opinion vs someone else's opinion is as big a matter now that

- God, I wish I could go back to even a year ago.

You will eventually have to
face your deepest fears, trust
someone or something (how about
your parents?)

choose the possibility of
finally recovering from this
agonizing state and returning
to a normal life or
ending with the result that
you think will happen anyway,

why not take that leap of faith
and choose the absolute belief
(in my mind) that you will become
normal again and begin to
have a real life,
NO MATTER HOW FRIGHTENING
THE CHOICE IS RIGHT NOW.

we've had seven years to
do that, I would have given
anything in the world to
enjoy being 21 but I'm
struggeling my guts out now
and if I could

talk more I would
but dad you can't say
this thing isn't ripping
me apart. How is anyone
going to help me if
I can barely go anywhere or
talk? come on, dad

All evidence suggests
the otherwise plus
obviously we dont have the
time we use too.
I mean look at me.

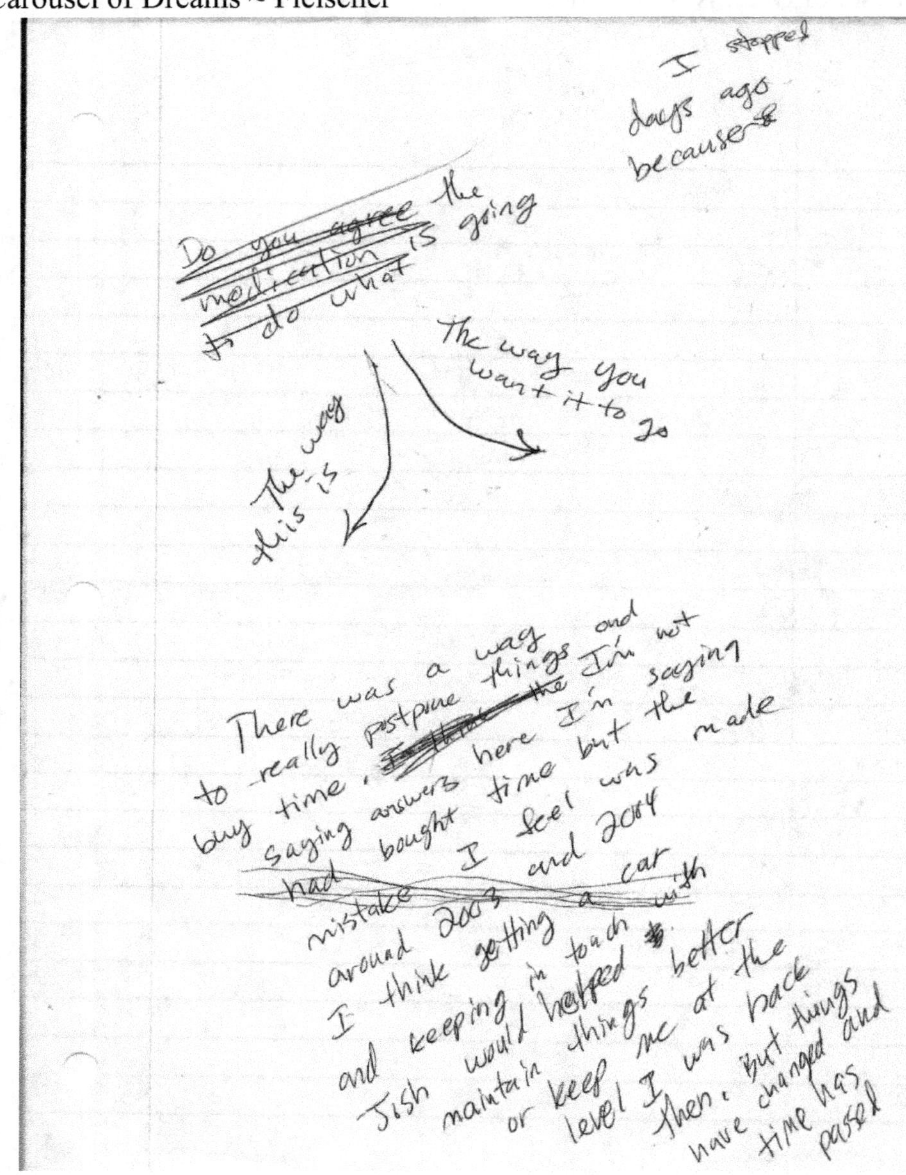

Do you agree the medication is going to do what

I stopped days ago because

The way you want it to go

The way this is

There was a way and time to really postpone things and buy time, here I'm not saying answers bought time but the I feel was made mistake around 2003 and 2004 I think getting a car and keeping in touch with Jish would helped maintain things better or keep me at the level I was back then. But things have changed and time has passed

my experience with medication
was never able to stop this
thing. my experience has been
generally negative.

I'd do anything to take
the edge off this problem;

if medication would take the
edge off my problem, but it
actually messes with me.

I need to be in <u>constant control</u>.
Medication messes with my ability
to do that.

Mom do you think when we went
to the park I look the same.

↘ Dad you keep focusing on the
medication but I told you that
their was other things that I
know made things much more
difficult like the choking about
2 or 3 weeks ago. (I literary
thought I was going to die) but
also the Tellys situation that happened
about a month / month and a half ago.
How could you sit and let Basta
say "Its medication only".
A lot of things tripped out my ability
to cope with the way it is which
had nothing to do with medication

- I was a fool for not taking my situation more seriously

- - To be as bold as to play with my problems like it was a game

- To not have reached out to Josh more over the time

- I think deep down I believed I could handle everything pretty well because at first I could (right after getting out of jail)

- I feel like I should have had more respect for my situation

- It made my situation worse on several occasion. The reason why is because at the center of my condition I have to be in control 24 hours a day to cope it. (which means no drinking, drugs, anything that causes a ~~disruption~~ disruption) ~~too~~ or else I get worse!!!
- The only drug I've ever been able to handle. is nicoteen. It gives a little comfort but not to. much to everwelm me. Thats all I've ever been able to handle since this all started.

- So what did pete say.
(It's okay you can tell
me)
Can I be honest
about something

- remember when I said
Im afraid something bad
going to happen to me.

- You know like I wont be adlo
do anything ~~~~~~

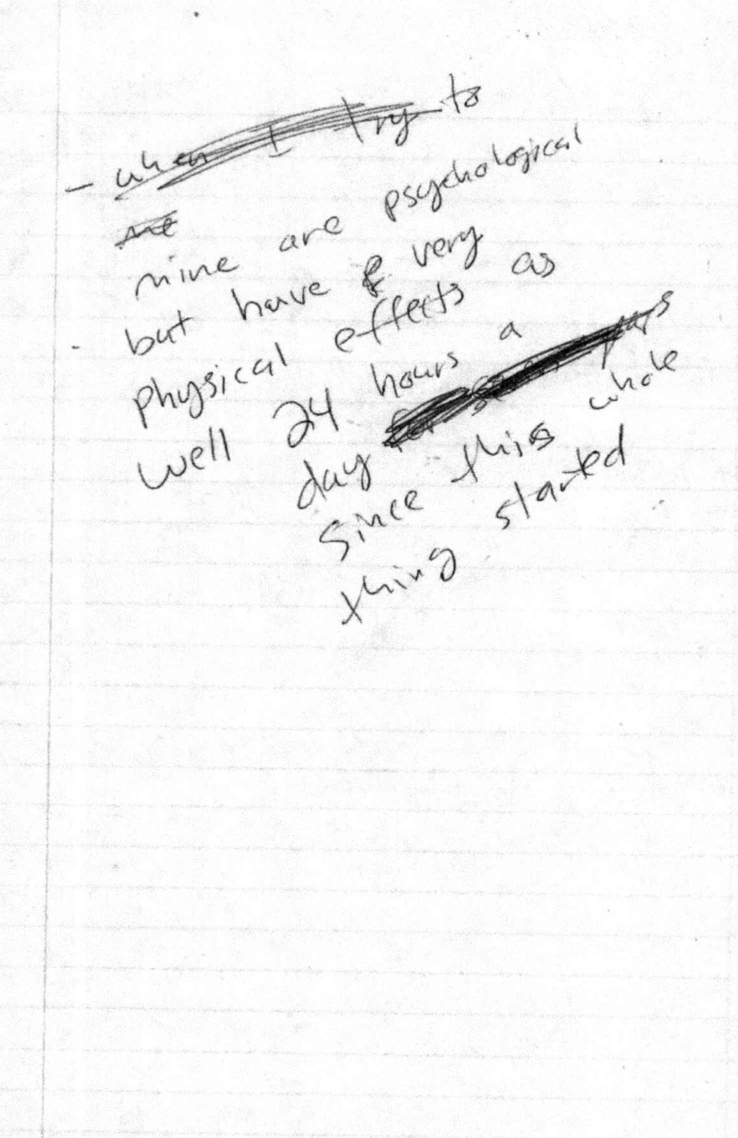
- when I try to
mine are psychological
but have of very
physical effects as
well 24 hours a
day since this whole
thing started

I'd say the best time dealing with this, in all 7 years, was right after Jail, For the first time I had no pressure to ~~try to work~~ and go to school because everyone knew that the situation was serious. Me and Josh kind of enjoyed a lot during that time, I kind of enjoyed a lot (compared to now). It was a game back then dealing with this thing. I was bored a lot, but I would Jump in the car, drive out

I really wish I could go back
to even right out of jail. I actually
kind of had some fun back then.
I went out with Josh several
times back then and even Barbie
As time went   with
whatever medication I was taking
the situation got harder

remember the skatebox in the backyard
I wanted to keep that to keep my
activitie up back then. For a courie years
Barbie wasn't here during the day and
Not having a skatebox plus no car during
that time was part of the problem.
The - Josh situation was part as well,
I really think that was the best
we could have done back. Im som
not saying solutions but I always new more
could be done to kind of postpone things.
But time has passed

\That was another sign things
were getting worse. I stopped
around 2004 because driving out
was getting to hard. And I couldnt
skate here.

- I'd say from the time I got out
of jail the first thing I started
struggelling with, after about a years.
was going to Hiedi & Hollies. I was
still driving a lot though, I even drove
to Hollywood, after Jail, to meet Diana
but as time went on. going to restraunts
skating, doing certain things got harder. That was all during the time of Basta

one thing I over the first 3 years and even the last couple years was that pushing wasn't exactly the thing to do. Coping with the way it is was a big part of it. Often times when I could cope with the way it is I didn't need anyone to push me cause I naturally could just go out. But the way it is was always getting more difficult so doing everything got more difficult. I specifically remember late 2004 and going does that the way it is got more difficult. That was just the enormous time thats gone by. I use to go out almost everyday with mom. Before that I would drive out almost everyday. with the first 3years I was pushing tremendously. certainly all of that would have added up to something. That's just not the way it worked

without some group-centered activity,
getting out with Rita or me or Barb doesn't
really do too much for your condition.
To get the Josh thing working again, the
social needs to be more peer-group (with same
kind of illnesses) centered. Otherwise there
is no lasting benefit.

This has nothing to do with that↑ but
I've always maintaind thing were getting
worse. I knew because I alot of things
I use to be able to do get harder.
I think it was hard for everyone to
See because it didn't really effect others
expect & I had to be drivin places more.
Now it really effected others. But thats
just the way its been going. The Josh
situation had a lot to do with that

social contact of some kind
is important.

Isolation is not good for
the   condition

My condition has always been
effected in that way but its gotten
worse over time. If you think about
it. Thats kind of how this started.
I was cut off socially my senior year
and it seemed like the drive to get
friends seem to be driving me into the
ground. People could say I was spiraling
In a manic situation on the surface
but inside thats the way it was.

The social contact, along with some other
things, will create a much better
situation.

I think the church situation
was the best this could of got I
thought that even then. I felt like
I sort of carved out an existance
back then, but a lots changed since then
lets just say I knew walking
away from the church but
was suicide I had to m

— Dad, You made a promise not
to let me get to that point,

Mom, Every Birthday I was always
not as good as before.

— What are you thinking
mom?

— I think 7 years is
plenty of time of
solve things
All the things I did in
the beginning plus these last
few years and nothing.

I think I would give anything in the world to have a different problem.

how

If Abby was like this
would you want Abby like this.

I

~~what do you~~ th

would you be to try this therapy
with large ~~too~~ doses of
~~ni~~ niacin (vitamin B.3)
which holds the possibility
of help? ~~to feeling~~
~~much~~

thats fine but
what next?
your clinging towards hope
you could do this till the
end of time. but I told you
years ago that we don't have
all the time in the world
Don't you think Basta could have recommended this.

Erik.. this is based
on 50 years of research
and Treatment in Canada.
with many successful cases!

↓ How much should I go thru before
   you guys believe me.

No, This situation just been
going downhill, I had some hope . thru
earlier.

I took Zyprexa for a very long
time Probably a year or 2

Yes But I was going downhill
the whole time. How do you that
   I got to this point.

I miss having hope dud.

↓ It was always going in this
direction its just the people
in the beginning, And my hardware,
postponed things.
You could read the letter I wrote from
the pawn shop thing and it all says
the same thing.

medication is going to do
whats its going to do. It
doesn't matter what I think.
I experience it and I tell
you if its working or not. You
Don't have to concivince of anything
What am I supposed to do though
when its not working and I cant
tell you.

Erik –

There is a very successful
Non-Drug therapy available
right now. I would like
to get you on it very soon
(a week or so)

It has proven to be
VERY EFFECTIVE !
for schizophrenia

Loner in Junior
Loser in high
Now half crazy as a virgin I die
Six feet five, ~~pretty~~ boy face
My only friends are shame and disgrace
Wish I could run, wish I could fly
: Stick a thousand needles in my eye
Wish I could run, wish I could love
So much anger, stuck in this mud,
Disturbances unreal, glued so fast
Wish I could change to break this old cast
wish I could change to begin the fade
Anger and rage at the things that have been made
Prisoner in chains, shackled to the floor
Will somebody please open the fucking door!
Wish I could love, wish I was a cat.
So much to prove, wish I was a cat
Much to late, wish I was a cat.